MW00453166

# A LISTENING LIFE

# A Listening Life

by Tracy Balzer

Pinyon Publishing
MONTROSE, CO

Copyright © 2011 by Tracy Balzer

All rights reserved. Except as permitted under the U.S. Copyright Act
of 1976, no part of this publication may be reproduced, distributed, or
transmitted in any form or by any means, or stored in a database or
retrieval system, without the prior written permission of the publisher,
except for brief quotations in articles, books, and reviews.

Back Cover Photograph of Tracy Balzer by Langley Balzer

Cover Design by Ashley Cecil
Book Design by Susan E. Elliott

First Edition: September 2011

Pinyon Publishing
23847 V66 Trail, Montrose, CO 81403
www.pinyon-publishing.com

Library of Congress Control Number: 2011935520
ISBN: 978-1-936671-04-5

# Acknowledgments

When listening is the topic of one's writing, the author should be prepared to listen to the wise counsel of others in the creative process. I am the grateful recipient of heaps of good counsel, without which I could not have begun nor completed this project.

First, I'd like to thank Jill Briscoe, who when asked whether I should add yet another book to the growing mountain of work on spiritual formation replied, "There can never be too many books on soul care." Her seasoned wisdom and warm encouragement (not to mention her exquisite British accent) gave me reason to try.

Lauren Winner's expert instruction and sincere interest helped me dive in. My friend and colleague Patty Kirk remains an invaluable source of expertise and feedback. Thanks also to her creative writing class at John Brown University for letting me read my work to them. Their comments are much appreciated. Friend and colleague, Kim Romig, also invited me to read to her university students, and my own section of Christian Formation students at John Brown University listened to my numerous readings. Patty Kirk routinely proclaims that reading one's work aloud is one of the surest ways to improve as a writer. I agree.

Many thanks to my editor, Gary Entsminger. It is a gift to work with someone who not only possesses the expertise to make my book better, but also the patience to encourage the author and engage the work itself. Thanks to my colleague, Todd Goehner, and the Graphics III students at John Brown University for their eagerness to collaborate on my project, and to Ashley Cecil for her cover design.

I am thankful to the sisters at St. Benedict's monastery in St. Joseph, Minnesota, whose Studium program granted me space and peace where I could write. Thanks to John Brown University for a grant that made that valuable time of writing possible. Thanks also to Shelly Casale and Kelley Smith for reading my early manuscript and contributing invaluable feedback and corrections.

Finally, I am part of a family whose love is a gift to me, whether I'm writing or not. Thanks and love to Cary, my husband, and to our daughter, Langley, as well as to Kelsey and Jordan, our daughter and son-in-law. They help me find appropriate measures of listening and laughter in my life.

*—for Sally*

*who has ears to hear*

# Contents

# Paying Attention

*A*n entire month on an Hawaiian island—this is the stuff of dreams. That dream became reality when we received a generous gift to help fund my husband's sabbatical. We packed our suitcases and relocated our family to the South Pacific for four blissful weeks.

Imagine this kind of paradise: no particular schedule, work responsibilities, or household clutter. Instead we enjoyed lazy afternoons in the sand and water with our two young daughters. We ate fresh pineapple for breakfast, lunch, and dinner. We watched the sky over the Pacific change from blue to pink to indigo every evening. Our lives slowed to a pace that was just what our weary minds and bodies needed.

My soul also needed some unhurried, extended time with God. As an active campus minister, mother, and wife, I longed for substantial time with God and the deep peace that always results. So every morning on Maui I got up a bit earlier than the rest of the family and took advantage of the quietest part of the day. First, I brewed fresh coffee and filled my oversized mug. With my free hand I grabbed my Bible, journal, and pen. Then I slipped on my flip flops and artfully managed to slide open the glass door. Stepping onto the dew-kissed lawn, I made my way to the seaside, where an empty lawn chair waited faithfully under a towering palm.

My spot on the beach definitely qualified as a "thin place"—an ancient Celtic concept of a location where the dividing line between heaven and earth seems tissue-paper thin. It was a stark contrast to the thickness that I experience in my daily life on the mainland. A typical morning at home would have me rushing to get my family out the door for work and school, passing out lunch bags, hunting for my wallet and keys, feeding the cat at the last second, and so on.

On Maui, I had time to slow the pace, to *pay attention*. I had time to drink in the beauty around me, to consider the changing spectrum of colors as the sun rose, illuminating one layer of the northern part of the island at a time, moving from top to bottom until the whole mountainside was awake in the light. I could sit still and watch the surface of the water slowly change color, reflecting the lavender of the morning sky, then gradually becoming its daily brilliant blue.

I watched a local family collect seaweed on the beach, noting their helpful interactions. I smiled as a retired couple walked by, hand-in-hand, and a man in a shiny black wet suit waded out into the shallows with his kayak. It was whale season, when the humpback females return to the island waters with their babies beside them. If I patiently watch and wait, I thought, I'll spot a revealing plume of spray or enormous tail flukes rising as if to wave to me before descending with a spectacular splash.

Scripture was a faithful teacher on those mornings, evidenced by the number of passages marked "Maui 2006" in the margins of my Bible. Meditating on scripture in an unhurried way was like sitting down to a delicious meal and savoring each bite. I wrote in my journal, carefully considering what was going on in both my heart and mind.

And I listened—to birdsong, to the breeze, to the waves rolling in and over the sand, line by line. I grew up in land-locked Colorado, so the crashing of waves has always had an hypnotic effect on me. On these mornings, however, something else beckoned. As each wave crashed and the water ebbed back, seaward, it left behind a space of strange quietness. It was that near-silence that caught my attention on those Maui mornings.

That stillness, almost startling, put all my senses on alert. I felt compelled to stop, look, and listen in full attention. I knew, of course, that what was coming next was another wave. But the blank space between each wave beckoned. Instead of anticipating the crash of the wave, I began to eagerly wait for that rhythmic yet quiet aftermath.

I have reflected on that silence-between-the-waves many times since my month of mornings on the beach. And when I do, I note the striking contrast to the typical pattern of my days, which are engulfed by technology, to-do lists, and business. I've grown weary of the noise and chaos; I want more of the quiet.

The many voices of our daily lives demand our attention. For those of us who want to live a spiritual life, for example, a Christian life in which Jesus stands at the center, those voices can be a significant obstacle. Perhaps we should ask, "In all of these voices, where is the Voice of Truth that we long to hear?" We believe that God speaks. But how do we discern his voice among so many? "Listen, listen to me, and eat what is good, and your soul will delight in the richest of fare," says the Lord through the prophet Isaiah. "Give ear and come to me; hear me, that your soul may live" (Isaiah 55:2-3).

This is an invitation to a feast that results in a delighted soul, a soul that is deeply satisfied. For this soul is a listening soul, dwelling in a listening life. This is a person who feasts upon the voice of God and *lives*.

We see this in the intimate relationship Jesus had with his Heavenly Father. Henri Nouwen says that Jesus was "all ear" for God. So we see in Jesus the living example of one who was always aware, always attentive to the Living Presence, always responding to the Voice. It is why Jesus said that all he needed to live was the Word of God (Matthew 4:4). The Word, the Voice, was his bread, "the richest of fare."

When Mary of Bethany chose to sit at Jesus' feet and give him her full attention, Jesus said she had chosen "what is better" (Luke 10:42). Jesus knows that a distracted life runs counter to a healthy one. He knows we too easily succumb to the many voices in our world, and that we neglect what is best, what we most need.

I want to make a significant contribution in the lives of the university students I work with. I also want to be attentive to the lives of university students. I also want to be attentive to the needs of my family—my husband, my teenage daughter, my newly married daughter and her husband. I want to be a good friend, to keep in touch with those far away, to pray faithfully for friends serving God around the world as they do what I will never have the courage to do. I want to make a positive, compassionate contribution to the world, even if it is something small, like sponsoring a child living in poverty. There is so much I want to do, and so much I feel I must do.

But such visions come at a cost if they drown out the voice of God. Even good things can distract us from what is very best, the better part that Mary chose at the feet of Jesus. For it's the better part that gives meaning and motivation to all of that *doing* in our lives.

I seek that attentive space, where I stop and listen to the silence between the waves.

Is such a listening life possible in our modern world? Can I learn to sort through the multitude of voices around me, discerning the True Voice of God in the midst of so many voices? The answer must be yes. For the Holy Spirit possesses his followers, and that Spirit speaks, guiding us into truth (John 16:6-13). Yes, a life of determined awareness of the voice and presence of God is indeed possible.

Not only is it possible, the pursuit of such a life is a delightful and more deeply meaningful one. When we are alert to the voice, to the living presence of God, we find that we've encountered something that transcends the superficial, the temporal. We discover a vast source of nourishment in a world that has the power to starve our souls. Once we have heard the voice of God, we will find it so satisfying that we will become, over time, "all ear" for him.

This kind of listening life—a life that deliberately makes space for God and pays attention to "what is better"—is a lifestyle that doesn't come naturally to me. I settle too often for the quick and easy answer to satisfy the moment, for what serves my own purposes best. I need God's help to be reoriented, to get the ears of my soul in tune with what God is up to, even though much of what I perceive is unseen and silent.

The world we live in places great value on productivity. We might be inclined to feel that seeking "what is better" is rather selfish. Our best defense is to return regularly to Jesus' instruction about what is most important, what is real, holy, and deep in life.

For we who have ears to hear, may the listening begin.

# Wonder

Years ago, when our kids were little, the comet Hale-Bopp appeared in the northwestern sky. We bundled up our two daughters and took them out to the back yard almost every night during the comet's two-week visit, just to see its dusty white tail glowing against the night sky. We stood on tip-toes and craned our necks to see over our neighbors' trees, passing binoculars back and forth to get the best view. We were mesmerized.

One night we received a double dose of astronomical wonder. While Hale-Bopp hovered in the north a total lunar eclipse occupied the south. Our girls were too young to understand the physics of these phenomena. They didn't care that the starry swoosh they saw at one end of the sky was a ball of rock and ice rocketing through space. Or that the earth can cast a shadow on the moon even when the sun is long gone from our view. But our exclamations of wonder were enough to tell them they were seeing something spectacular and special.

My husband, Cary, and I have tried our best to make room for awe in our daughters' lives. We believe that collecting experiences is more important than collecting material items. So on one of those comet nights, Cary cleverly maneuvered Kelsey's bed 180 degrees around so she could look out the window at Hale-Bopp before falling asleep. I stood silently in her doorway, charmed by Cary's effort to enhance Kelsey's encounter with the comet. I carved the image of our nine-year-old daughter in my memory, as she lay in her turned-around bed gazing at a comet framed in the window above her feet.

Theologians apply the term "general revelation" to anything in the created universe that reveals truth about God to us. This contrasts with "special revelation" which refers to the Holy Scripture. I understand the need for the word "special" when referring to the Bible. But the word "general" seems tame, banal in reference to something as spectacular as a comet or an eclipse. "The heavens declare the glory of God," wrote the Psalmist (Psalm 19:1), providing a fitting description of Hale-Bopp's purpose in the sky. "General" by definition, perhaps. But "special" in every other way.

The mysteries of outer space have fascinated me for as long as I can remember. I was a young girl when I watched Neil Armstrong's historic moonwalk on our black and white television set. His giant leap lured me into reading books about space. The pages of one book I ordered through my school's book club—innocuously titled *Stars*—became disconnected from the spine after my repeated viewing of the glossy photographs. The Horsehead Nebula. Alpha Centauri. The Milky Way. Saturn. These majestic celestial bodies existed and moved in the unfathomable expanse of space for millennia before any sentient being discovered them. They still make vivid appearances in the skies of my dreams. These heavenly bodies, so distant from me in physical proximity, have found a permanent place in my consciousness, speaking to me of something beyond myself that is incomprehensible.

The Psalmist wrote: "Day after day they pour forth speech; night after night they display knowledge. There is no speech or language where their voice is not heard." When we listen to that "voice" in the heavens that declares God's grandeur in every language, our instinctive reaction is that of wonder. A circle of divine communication is complete: God created the universe and called it good. His creation continually declares his glory, and we who witness that declaration respond in praise with the "Amen!" of wonder—*a response that is good for the soul.*

Field trips were highlights of my elementary school years. These events required written permission from my mother and promised the adventure of riding in a school bus (usually I walked to school). I especially liked our trips to the Denver Planetarium. To recline in the black polyester chairs of the planetarium auditorium and look up at the great dome above seemed a preparation for interstellar travel. I could have been sitting behind the controls of the Starship Enterprise. The verbal instructions from the unseen guide ("Once the program has begun, you may not exit the auditorium") signaled our take-off. An impenetrable darkness filled the room, and with chills raising the hair on my neck, I became convinced that I was not long for this earth—which was *excellent* news. I held my breath as we flew through galaxies, witnessing the birth of stars, avoiding vaporization as we slalomed through an asteroid field. Small tears formed in the corners of my eyes, and I gripped the armrests of my chair as we returned once again to Earth.

Now, reflecting, I believe I experienced something akin to worship in those flights and an overwhelming sense of the greatness of God. Even a simulated encounter with the wonders of the universe can connect us to a profoundly creative Creator.

This realization nourishes us when we are in doubt. Wonder reminds us that there is more to life than what we can see and touch. It yanks us out of a self-absorption that is life-taking rather than life-giving. To live without wonder is to be subject to the gravitational pull of a spiritual black hole that strips life of meaning and sucks us into a vortex from which it seems impossible to escape.

An experience of wonder changes the lenses through which we view life. A colleague at the university where I teach leads short expeditions out to the country, telescopes in tow, for the purpose of introducing others to what he calls "God's Wow." I've been on these expeditions, and it's not only thrilling to see Saturn's rings or Jupiter's moons, but also to experience them with friends as they too put their eyes to the lens. On a country hill at midnight, we are a holy congregation offering our collective praises. I leave with gratitude and a broader perspective on life, encouraged by the reminder that the God who balances planets also checks the forces that threaten to pull my life apart.

Our astonishment is not limited to encounters with outer space. The earth abounds with natural wonders. I once visited the foothills of Mt. St. Helens, soon after its powerful eruption. I was stunned by the gray dust that suddenly covered what once was a perfect, cone-shaped mountain. A multitude of trees had snapped and now lay like a child's pick-up-sticks.

I've heard humpback whales singing to each other as I held my breath in deep water beneath the turquoise

Pacific, privileged to eavesdrop on these splendid creatures, to hear their sub-marine conversations. I've walked in trepidation twenty meters across a rope suspension bridge linking the rocky mainland of Northern Ireland to the tiny island of Carrick, resisting the temptation to close my eyes, and choosing instead to embrace the tension between uncertainty and safety. These experiences take my breath away.

My family has learned to love wildlife, especially the colorful songbirds that annually visit our country home. In our first spring in Arkansas, we hung a bird feeder on our back deck. That first day of April I stood at the kitchen window. The feeder swung gently, covered with a dozen bright yellow birds I didn't recognize. So I set the pan I was scrubbing in the sink and took our copy of *Birds of North America* off a nearby shelf. Goldfinches, I read, and they usually arrived in our area of Arkansas in early April. Ours were right on schedule. Now we look forward to seeing them every spring. And they seldom come alone, but are accompanied by bluebirds, cardinals, woodpeckers, and stunning scarlet tanagers. Each of them beckons us to come away, even if briefly, from our current tasks.

Our wildlife visitors also include deer, possums, and quirky armadillos. A great blue heron flies over regularly, headed toward the nearest marsh, and every December we search the sky for the majestic bald eagles that nest here in winter. We watch for the campus woodchuck family on our way to work. Hummingbirds arrive each spring to buzz at our windows, pestering us to fill their feeders with bright red sugar water. Each of these encounters contributes to my sense of wonder, that the Creator of these marvels is the same

One who astonished us with a comet for a few weeks one summer.

I am learning that poets can help us appreciate wonder.

The poet, Luci Shaw, helped me think about poetry differently, to appreciate the hard work that goes into making a poem sound right. In a class of hers I attended, Luci often read her poems to us. She taught us to watch for what she calls "the numinous," bits of creation filled with meaning beyond itself. For example, in her poem "Overhead," from *Harvesting Fog*:

> The sun is a slow gong
> in a brass bowl, the moon also
>
> rings her bell against
> the indigo steel of the night sky.
>
> By painting, Emily Carr
> decoded heaven as coastline
>
> vast bays of ripped blue
> and Vincent drew his circles
>
> tighter than the tattered orbits
> of his own life.
>
> Art like that
> irrational and entire
>
> is all perception
> the surreal turning real:
>
> how poets sift what they see
> into what they feel,
>
> pulling new pieces of heaven
> into view.

When I was first getting to know Cary's family, they invited me to join them for Sunday afternoon drives in the rugged Cascade Mountains of Washington. During one outing we came upon a dramatic waterfall cascading through craggy rocks, and one of us spontaneously cheered in response. From then on, we all seemed to have a heightened awareness of the natural wonders around us: a snow-capped peak, a raging river, you name it, and those wonders would be echoed by more of our applause. Even now that our daughters are grown, our family still acts as if we're seeing these wonders of nature for the first time. When Kelsey returned from her semester abroad in Oxford last year, she said her friends there told her she clapped a lot. Which made us laugh, knowing it was true of all of us. I imagine Kelsey clapping as she rambled through the English countryside or gaped at the glorious architecture of Christopher Wren.

I want my children, my students, my*self,* to feel comfortable applauding the wonders of our lives, to be listeners to that "general revelation" that is anything but general. Wonder-filled experiences alert us to transcendence, reminding us that God works creatively within us.

Mysterious objects in the sky have long fascinated humanity. One famous incident involved the "magi" of early Christianity. What were they wondering when they saw that extraordinary star in the east? Surely they experienced something "numinous," something unlike anything they'd seen before. This star spoke to them. It had a message, and they listened. The heavens declared the glory of God, so powerfully that they knew they must follow the star. They believed God had put his star in the sky, and the magi responded, kneeling at the feet of the Christ Child.

The Psalm writer articulated this wonder long, long ago:

> When I consider your heavens,
> the work of your fingers,
> the moon and the stars,
> which you have set in place,
> what is man that you are mindful of him,
> the son of man that you care for him?
> (*Psalm 8:3-4*)

I believe our attraction to wonder is something we all share. Bruce Demarest, in *Seasons of the Soul: Stages of Spiritual Development*, says that we are "searching for relationship with something or Someone larger than [ourselves] that will ease the dullness of daily life and energize the soul. Christians," he continues, "hunger for more intimate experience of Jesus Christ and greater awareness of the Spirit's ministry within."

Those who give attention to the wondrous share a kinship with the magi of old. An even greater kinship with the wondrous God of the universe awaits us.

# Illumination

Since I was very young I've been fascinated by letter shapes and have tried to copy them, from elegant script to calligraphic italic to the rounded uncials of the earliest sacred manuscripts. The thought of spending my days in a monastic scriptorium, painstakingly copying the scriptures by candlelight, appeals to my romantic tendencies.

The monastic history of Ireland and Scotland has drawn me to back to the British Isles, especially to Iona, the tiny Scottish isle where Celtic monks created the glorious *Book of Kells*. This collection of gospels—"illuminated" because of its intricate illustrations embellished with gold leaf—is one of the finest and best preserved manuscripts of medieval Europe. Trinity College in Dublin, Ireland secured its safety a number of years ago, and it is now enshrined in an exquisite public exhibit. Each time I'm in Dublin, I happily plop down ten Euros to see it again.

About ten years ago, the monks of St. John's Abbey in Minnesota commissioned calligrapher Donald Jackson (a scribe to Queen Elizabeth, no less) to create a new illuminated manuscript of the entire Bible. I wanted to know more. My inquiry led me to the Hill Memorial Manuscript Library on the campus of St. John's University where the finished project resides. I had to see this art of illumination for myself.

On an unseasonably cool July afternoon I descended the stairs to the lower level of the library where a selection of the St. John's Bible original is displayed. Standing behind an information desk, a bright university student offered to take my friend and me into the exhibit. "You came at a great time," she said. "We're currently displaying the Gospels and Acts, which are among the most illuminated of the whole Bible." I got excited and even a little smug—I was going to see some of the most beautiful pages of the whole lot: the most illuminated.

Our guide led us to the room where the work awaited our viewing, each page affixed behind glass and lit to bring attention to an array of gold-leafed illumination. Sure enough, the artists had run riot with gold, knowing just where to apply its brilliance to highlight words and illustrations. The glory of Jesus, the "light of the world," shone through earthy paper, ink, and mineral.

For the calligrapher, "illumination" means "the reflection of light on gold." Applying whisper-thin sheets of gold leaf to a specially prepared surface gives a scribe the power not only to draw attention to an element of the work, but also to assign royalty, divinity, or transcendence to a word or illustration. The gilded element commands its viewers to give it special notice, perhaps even honor.

I like the way "illumination" sounds. It brings to mind a magician's velvet curtain, drawn back with a dramatic, sweeping motion to reveal a grand mystery. Or it conjures images of glowing faces and clothes, like Moses coming down from the mountain after his one-on-one conversation with Yahweh. Illumination. Light, Reflection. And we, like Moses, are changed by that.

Once Jesus took his friends up to a mountain. Peter, James, and John surely had no idea of the magnitude of what was about to happen. Matthew says that Jesus' "face shone like the sun, and his clothes became as white as the light" (Matthew 17:2). Mark says "His clothes became dazzling white, whiter than anyone in the world could bleach them" (Mark 9:3). It was as if God, the great Illuminator, touched Jesus with gold leaf so that he might stand out and command attention over and above the rest of creation.

Peter's response was to *do* something, to create, to be productive, to get in on the act. I recognize this impulse, as an urge to maximize something by converting it into a sermon illustration or object lesson. I can just imagine Peter's thoughts, "This is incredible! Now what can we *do* with it?"

While Peter was verbalizing his grand idea, God interrupted him.

"While he was still speaking, a bright cloud enveloped them, and a voice from the cloud said, 'This is my Son, whom I love; with him I am well pleased. Listen to him!'" *This is the point,* God was saying, *listen to Jesus. If there's something more to be done, you'll find out soon enough.*

When our daughters, Kelsey and Langley, were quite young, we went to visit their great-grandparents in an Oklahoma nursing home. We sat together on upholstered couches and chairs in the center of a large reception room while other residents shuffled in and out. At some point I realized that Kelsey, then eight years old, was not with us. I wasn't terribly concerned, knowing she couldn't have gone far. But my "mother's eye" began scanning the area around us to be sure.

Then I spotted her: she was on the far side of the room, smiling as she stood in front of an elderly woman sitting in a wheelchair and looking intently into her eyes. They were clearly having a friendly conversation, even though Kelsey could have only known her as a stranger. The old woman smiled broadly in response. As I took in the curious scene, I had the strange impression that Kelsey's face was glowing, almost literally. For a moment, it appeared that she was wearing the face of Jesus as she tenderly loved this woman, a stranger.

This was a simple experience of illumination, an illustration of the ways God reaches us through otherwise ordinary events. When Jesus taught his disciples, his lessons featured every-day events—like walking through a field, or noticing who's putting what into the temple offering, or watching birds fly. Yet each became moments of enlightenment. In the nursing home that day, God, the Artist, laid down a bit of gold on the face of a child, speaking to me about what it means to love as Christ loves.

Illumination comes in the midst of frustration. Even when nothing's glowing, when no epiphanies seem possible, something worth waiting for emerges. God's method of gaining our attention often takes us by surprise, like a fleck of gold on a dark page.

Years ago, on our first visit to Arkansas, I learned that a beautiful chapel had been designed so that visitors had a sense of being in the woods while still being within the shelter of the small sanctuary. I planned to spend time there for prayer and solitude.

I drove to the glade where the chapel sat among towering pines. The air was cool, the sky overcast. The chatter of cardinals and blue jays accompanied me as I walked the curving trail up to the double doors of the chapel. Gingerly I stepped inside, delighted to discover that the chapel was empty—I was the only person there. I looked for and found the right spot for my hour of quiet, halfway back and halfway between the center aisle and the huge, clear windows on the side. I sat, released a muffled sigh of delight, closed my eyes, and breathed in the delicious silence.

Two minutes elapsed and I heard the tall wooden doors behind me creak; a white-haired man stepped in and slowly walked up to the front near the altar. "No problem," I thought. "I can share this quiet space with someone else."

But rather than stopping to sit in one of the front pews, he kept walking. He continued up to the platform and sat at the baby grand piano. I sat dumbstruck: he raised his hand to the keys and sharply struck two dissonant notes, together, over and over. Then he played two different and comparably dissonant notes. Then two high notes an octave apart. Repeat.

It was piano-tuning day at the chapel.

I instinctively went into internal battle-mode. I was angry at my rotten luck and furious with Satan, who clearly was partnering with this piano tuner to conspire against me. I was a bit miffed at God for not protecting our time together.

Then came the directive: *Just sit tight and wait. There may be something in this for you.* It wasn't an audible instruction, but a clear one nonetheless.

I fidgeted in my seat, huffed and puffed in frustration, and relented. I sat as still as I could and waited reluctantly, but I did it. I watched and listened to all of those dissonant, jarring notes, sounds that produced precisely the opposite effect on my soul that I'd been hoping for. But I watched and listened to the piano tuner work his magic, as if that's what I had come for in the first place.

Every once in awhile, instead of hearing dissonant notes, I found myself directed to the bits of dissonance in my own life—to the discordance that had pervaded our family's life for the past two years. I realized there were *notes* in our lives that were bumping against each other, and as I listened to the piano tuner's notes in the chapel, echoing my own, I began to understand their origin. The dissonance in our lives came from *where* we were and *what* we were doing.

*Where* we were was far from family—parents, grandparents, brothers, sisters. We enjoyed living in the beautiful Pacific Northwest, our home for many years. But it lost its charm as, one by one, our family members moved away. We longed for familial relationships.

*What* we were doing was no longer matching who God called us to be. Both Cary and I had longed to be in university ministry ever since we'd been college students. Our years of pastoral ministry in the local church had taught us a lot, but with each passing year our desire to work in Christian higher education increased.

That piano tuner, the one that had disrupted my best-laid plans for silence and solitude, had helped illuminate truth to me, the truth of the dissonance in my life and how important it was to pay attention to it. I left the chapel, and in the weeks following, the dissonance of life grew ever-louder. For months we asked God to replace it with harmony, to allow those incongruent notes to resolve into something that was more pleasing to our ears.

After two years of waiting and praying, the dissonance was indeed resolved: a Christian university, one that was much closer to our extended family, hired us both.

I made other sojourns to the chapel during that first Arkansas visit, each of them filled with the silence and solitude I had originally hoped for. But it's funny how the Day of the Piano Tuner is the one I most remember, the day the dissonance in my life was illuminated.

Scripture is illuminating, if we are keen to pay attention. The ancient practice of *lectio divina* is gaining support from contemporary evangelicals, thanks to the work of folks like Eugene Peterson and Richard Foster and others who teach and write about it. This discipline of sacred reading, of digesting scripture rather than dissecting it, has become a lifeline for me. In *lectio divina* we engage the illuminated word of God in small portions that speak huge truths. Author Jan Johnson uses the word "shimmer" when describing how the Scriptures can catch our attention in particular ways. Engaging in *lectio divina* opens our eyes and ears to the Word as God illuminates it for our notice.

At the end of each summer, before our students arrive on campus, our entire faculty and staff get together to worship and celebrate the good things God has done. This year our guest was author and journalist Andy Crouch. We invited him to talk to us about his popular book, *Culture Making*. Imagine our surprise when instead of taking the podium to speak, he sat down at the grand piano and began to play.

He settled into a lazy bass-driven melody, that exquisite balance of lead, rhythm, bass that all music lovers adore. And then his voice began, introducing a traditional gospel song:

> Over my head
> I hear music in the air
>
> Over my head
> I hear music in the air
>
> Over my head
> I hear music in the air
>
> There must
> be a God somewhere

So Andy repeated that song, inviting us to sing along. With each repetition our energy increased, until Andy coaxed us to clap on the off-beat. Then like a good choir director, he urged us to put more emphasis on certain words, to sharply enunciate the words "music in the air," to end the word "must" crisply, and to let the word "God" expand and fill the room. Andy illuminated that song for us, making it a vehicle for our attention to truth. Singing became a *lectio divina* experience.

Gerard Manley Hopkins' poem, "God's Grandeur," reminds us that divine electricity surges all around us and is deserving of our meditation, and our contemplation.

> The world is charged with the grandeur of God.
> It will flame out, like shining from shook foil;

Only rarely will we be the recipients of something very obvious and aflame, like a burning bush. But frequently the Word of God comes to life, glowing on the printed page, or in a congregational song, or on the face of a child.

# Pain and People

C. S. Lewis said, "God whispers to us in our pleasures, speaks in our conscience, but shouts in our pains: it is his megaphone to rouse a deaf world."

But when I experience pain or trauma, God's voice isn't loud and clear. I don't hear him. When I'm in crisis, God's voice becomes much more muddled. It's like I'm under anesthetic with senses completely dulled. Someone is trying to wake me. I hear only garbled syllables, and I am numb.

My husband, Cary, was the pastor of a small congregation in Washington State for five years. A transition came when he accepted a position at a larger church in Redmond, east of Seattle. It was a timely change, and we knew we'd done what we could for our little church. But then came news that we'd waited and prayed for: I was finally pregnant with our second child. Everything seemed good and right, and we soaked up the thrill that comes with new adventures on the horizon.

We enthusiastically anticipated our first Sunday at our new church. On the Saturday morning of that weekend, Cary woke up with strange symptoms: his entire right leg was numb. Not the needles-and-pins kind of numb that meant it was "asleep." He couldn't feel *anything*. We had returned from a trip the day before, so we assumed he'd pinched a nerve while hauling our luggage around. That Saturday afternoon ignoring his leg's numbness, he mowed the lawn, undeterred by the mysterious symptoms.

On Sunday morning the alarm rang, waking us for an exciting day at our new church, and Cary said to me, "My other leg is numb, too." To say the least, that was troubling. But our hopes buoyed us for the day, and we tried not to be frightened. I tried calmly to suggest that Cary go on to the first service at church, and I would call a doctor. Four-year-old Kelsey and I would join him for the second service.

When the doctor answered the phone and I reported the mysterious symptoms, he responded with a question: "Where's your husband now?" "Oh, he went to work," I answered as calmly as my voice would allow. I received a chilly response. Apparently Cary's symptoms were more serious than we thought, and going to work in such a condition was a rather naïve thing for him to do. I promised the doctor we'd meet him at his clinic immediately after church.

Our new congregation lovingly welcomed us that morning, including a "pounding" of all kinds of food items to fill our pantry. Smiling women presented themselves to me as prospective friends, expressing their delight when I told them I was three months pregnant.

After an hour or so of shaking hands, I slipped away for a bathroom break where I discovered an alarming symptom of my own, the one that every newly pregnant woman dreads—a spot of blood, telling me things may not be all right. I forced my own physical concern to the back of my mind, convinced it was an isolated occurrence, and gave my attention to Cary's situation.

Cary and I said goodbye to our new church friends and went straight to the clinic where the doctor thoroughly examined him and blurted out his curt hypothesis: Cary was presenting symptoms of multiple sclerosis. Now I was the one who felt numb, unable to respond. Before I knew it, Cary was admitted to the hospital.

Over the next two days and a series of tests, Cary's diagnosis of MS was confirmed. We received it in disbelief; the only person we'd ever known with MS was a young man confined to a wheelchair and needing constant care. To think that Cary, my strong, young husband, could someday be in the same situation made me feel light-headed and nauseated. On Tuesday of that week we checked him out of the hospital with a starchy prognosis from the neurologist: *MS is a cruel disease ... there's no way of knowing what it will do ... it may be bad, it may not be so bad ... call me if it gets bad.*

It did get bad, and rapidly, but not for Cary—for me. Within twenty-four hours of Cary's discharge from the hospital, I was likewise admitted, the spotting not being a fluke after all. My obstetrician conducted an ultrasound and gave me the distressing news: there was no heartbeat, I'd miscarried our baby. They whisked me into the operating room to remove the lifeless tissue from my uterus. The feeling of being under anesthetic was now literally true as well as metaphorically. I was completely unable to make any sense of these events, and God's voice seemed particularly dull. In the midst of the fog, I wondered whose life I was living.

I lived in that fog for the next three or four months. I was functional but fearful. While small Kelsey instinctively lined up stones on our back fence as a memorial to our baby, I waited for Cary to tell me that the feeling in his legs had returned. It was many weeks before he could. And though the symptoms were gone, the fear of the future remained. MS is a capricious disease.

The week after Christmas, I stood in the returns line at a department store with about a hundred other people. I stood there, mindlessly waiting for my turn at the counter, when I was suddenly jolted to attention by the images around me. In front of me a young woman held a beautiful, pink baby girl. Behind me a middle-aged woman leaned on a cane to walk. She bore no evidence of an injury, no bandages or cast. So I jumped to the conclusion she had MS. I stood looking at these two women, flesh-and-blood illustrations of the big questions in my life. Would secondary infertility and miscarriage continue to prevent us from having a second child? Would MS steal the vitality and mobility from my husband?

Those questions had haunted me for months, and suddenly, here in the returns line, they materialized before my eyes. I was stuck in the middle of them, wondering if God was in the line, too, or if maybe he was elsewhere, shopping.

The gospel story, found in Mark 2, of the paralyzed man whose friends carried him to Jesus is one I ruminate on frequently. Those friends were so determined to get this man to Jesus that when a crowd of people stood in their way, they entered the house via the scenic route, tearing a hole in the roof right over Jesus' head and lowering their friend down. This is a profound image of the power of intercession. When we are "paralyzed" and it seems impossible for us to get to Jesus, we may discover that the shoulders and prayers of determined friends are the most effective means of transportation.

Looking back on those scary days of MS and miscarriage, I can see ways in which the pain we experienced ushered me into a new way of listening. I began to hear God through people—faithful friends bearing the image of God were, for me, his messengers of love when his voice otherwise seemed indiscernible. They did the praying for me, which was good because the only prayer I could pray was a one-liner, over and over: *Lord Jesus, take away my fear.* A delicious meal would arrive at our door, and I felt carried. My friend Sally, a dental professional, prayed for me daily (and still does) as she cleaned her patients' teeth, carrying me to Jesus. And every week my circle of praying friends would carry me on my figurative stretcher and lower me down to his feet.

One of my favorite movies is *Lars and the Real Girl*. In one powerful scene a few of the community women come to the home of a friend who had died. They step into the kitchen, deposit their hot-dish offerings for the grieving family, and then proceed to sit down and take out their knitting. When asked by another visitor what they are doing, they answer, expressionless, "We're sitting." Coming and sitting, silent but present, is what they did when someone was hurting, and it was enough.

A few years later, after our hopes for a second child were realized with Langley's birth, Cary experienced a particularly nasty MS episode that involved partially losing his eyesight. His neurologist prescribed a powerful round of intravenous steroids to halt the progress of the attack and preserve his eyesight. The side effects of the treatment were abominable, causing random, painful muscle spasms and robbing him of sleep at night.

After one of those treatments, we left the hospital hopeful the steroids would do their work. But we dreaded the next few days of the chaos they would wreak on his body. We felt emotionally spent, physically and spiritually fatigued. So we did the natural thing: we stopped for comfort food.

As we sat in our booth eating fried chicken and mashed potatoes, a bus load of young African Americans entered the restaurant and began to sing. I looked at Cary in disbelief. A gospel choir had come to Boston Market, not only to eat, but to sing? I became convinced it was for us. Because really, is there anything more uplifting than a gospel choir? Their voices soared, they swayed back and forth, some lifting their hands to the sky. It was as if God surveyed the situation and asked himself, "Let's see, what would the Balzers really like right now?" The Holy Spirit used a hungry choir on tour to raise up a couple of weary souls. We politely thanked them later as we walked out the door (we did not offer to sing for them), but I will always regret not telling them more precisely why their song was such a gift to us.

I remember the choir singing "I Believe I Can Fly," which usually, in an unforgivable expression of musical snobbery, I would write off as sentimental fluff. That day my attitude was different.

Now and then God brings these kinds of friends my way to help me better decode his words in the midst of my pain. They are part of a global clan of souls who, knowingly or unknowingly, are used by God. Such folk come across our path for what appears to be one reason: to carry us for a while. It's what we used to call a "divine appointment."

So if I had the audacity to challenge C. S. Lewis, I might say, "Although pain could be God's megaphone, it's often *people* he uses in our pain to get our attention."

# Persistence, "Starry Night"

*A* few summers ago I attended a week-long professional conference at Yale University. I was there to speak and also to enjoy invigorating conversations, corporate worship, and thought-provoking teaching. The days were stimulating. I made new friends, and my mind hummed with new ideas.

But half-way through the week, I knew I had to get away and make space for myself, or there would be negative ramifications to deal with (mostly, I knew I would get really cranky). I've learned this about myself in my adult years; I can behave like an extravert when needed, but I'm an introvert at my core. Fortunately, the conference planners had scheduled a "Sabbath afternoon" for that Wednesday. It gave me permission to do exactly what I needed to do.

I'd never been to Connecticut before, so I used part of that afternoon to wander around the city of New Haven. It is charming: gothic architecture, tree-lined avenues, and colonial houses. The lovely surroundings helped me to slow down, even in the midst of a busy college town's activity. An impulsive stop in an Irish shop for tea and a scone didn't hurt either.

I noticed banners hanging from the light posts hailing a special exhibition at the Yale Art Gallery. That was appealing enough, as art galleries are splendid places to enjoy some solitude. But these banners shouted to me: Vincent van Gogh's celebrated painting, "Starry Night," was there on loan from the Museum of Modern Art. Since it's one of the world's most recognized paintings, I decided I should go see it. Truth be told, I think I mostly wanted to *say* I'd seen it, so I could tell my friends I'd seen this world-famous painting, the way some people I know make a point of having seen the "Mona Lisa" when visiting Paris. Although everybody knows what it looks like, there's something about being able to say you stood in its presence that seems impressive.

I walked up the stairs and through the doors of the gallery and was met by a smiling young woman who handed me my free entrance ticket. Not surprisingly, "Starry Night" was a popular attraction, so I had to wait for my assigned time slot before I could see it. When that time finally arrived, I took the stairs up to the third floor, gave my ticket to the attendant, and rounded the corner where the painting hung.

I was astonished. The real "Starry Night" was unlike any reproduction I'd ever seen. I wondered if the attendant heard me gasp.

The colors were dazzling: deep midnight blue, egg-yolk yellow, a great swirl of brilliant white. The texture of the artist's deliberate strokes reached out and made the painting come alive. Its beauty shocked me out of all my preconceptions. It was magnetic, and it held me there, transfixed, for I don't know how long. I knew I must return and see it again.

And I did, the next afternoon, and again the next day when I brought my journal with me and sat down on the bench in front of the painting. I couldn't escape the impression that this painting was speaking. I let "Starry Night" do the talking.

I was quickly drawn again to the pure white, swirling, movement the artist placed in the skies above a sleeping town, motion that I could only imagine to be the divine activity of God. I sat and pondered this active God, always up to something, always creating, always watching, even at night while I am asleep, oblivious, below. The poetry of Psalm 121 came to mind:

> He will not let your foot slip—
>     he who watches over you will not slumber;
> Indeed, he who watches over Israel
>     will neither slumber nor sleep.
> The LORD watches over you—
>     the LORD is your shade at your right hand.
> The sun will not harm you by day,
>     nor the moon by night.

Through van Gogh's brushstrokes, I saw the world as quiet, still, while God above was the busy one. By contrast, our modern earthly existence is too often chaotic, a frenzy of activity, while we imagine God resting placidly in the vacuum of space with not much more to do than wait, unswervingly patient for us to give him the time of day. Harried earth below, serene skies above.

"Starry Night" gives a different vision, one that is both perceptive and biblical. In van Gogh's village, the people are still, and God above is active, vigorous, and creative. In van Gogh's colorful skies we see the glory and power of a God who works in ways that allows the villagers to rest. As I pondered this, "Starry Night" spoke: *Do you truly believe God is working on your behalf? Or do you feel the need to step in and fix things yourself?*

Another feature of the painting is van Gogh's dark cypress tree in the corner of his painting—a strange alien plant, looming large. I say "alien" because van Gogh used long, smooth strokes to create it, setting it apart from the rest of the painting's short, choppy patterns. This is an element I hadn't noticed when looking at reproductions. But now those long alien strokes drew my attention to the plant, dark and muted as it was in contrast to the luminous skies above. "Starry Night" spoke again: *What is the alien plant in your world that is distracting you from God's creative work around you?*

One of my great weaknesses is the abject intimidation I feel regarding personal finances. I have always been terrible at math; numbers mystify me, make me feel stupid. And, grateful as I am for it, I really don't like money. In moments of childishness, I wish it just didn't exist. Because if we didn't have to mess with money, I wouldn't have to constantly feel guilty for how badly I deal with it. I'm so inept at keeping records and budgeting that my stomach constricts into a mass of nerves whenever it comes time for me to check our accounts online. Numbers and I are not friends. They are out to get me. Behold my alien plant.

Money and numbers intimidate me. And that intimidation diabolically distracts me from the many blessings that bring so much beauty into my life. I cringe as I watch this dark thing grow bigger and bigger toward the end of every month. The fact is, it really isn't money or numbers that make up that alien plant: it is *fear*. Fear that I will be irresponsible with the gifts God has given me. Fear that I will make costly mistakes. Fear that I am a hindrance in our family to the financial stability I see in other families around us. I'm afraid of failure.

"Starry Night" required three visits from me because there were a few things I needed to hear, truths I needed to see. Although its image was familiar to me, I'd never really *seen* it before. I've been too content with a superficial vision of this painting, of what I *thought* it looked like. The Yale Art Gallery gave me the opportunity to genuinely encounter, to experience, to meditate upon it. To let it teach me.

I cannot presume to fully know or understand something, just because it is familiar to me. How arrogant to think that there is no more to be discovered, particularly when it comes to matters of the Spirit. "How deep, the Father's love for us, how vast beyond all measure," the hymn sings. There is always more to be discovered.

For years I have routinely kept the shades of my office closed. This creates a darker than desired atmosphere, but the view outside my office window is less than aesthetically pleasing. I decided long ago that the image of automobiles lined up on asphalt does not help me shape the restful environment I wish to create for my student visitors. So, closed they have remained.

That is, until recently, a beautiful late summer day, when I had the urge to let some sunlight in. I opened the shades just a bit, not only letting in the sun, but giving me a peek at something outside that shocked me: a tall, leafy tree had grown just outside my window!

How long has it been growing there? Months? A year? Clearly, I had made the assumption that there was nothing worth seeing outside my window. Now a flourishing golden raintree obliterates the otherwise unattractive parking lot and fills my window with lovely green leaves and papery seed pods that look like Japanese lanterns. What other delights am I missing because I have made foolish assumptions? What gifts have I not received because I refuse to take the time to look?

"Superficiality is the curse of our age," says Richard Foster in *Celebration of Discipline*. "The doctrine of instant satisfaction is a primary spiritual problem. The desperate need today is not for a greater number of intelligent people or gifted people, but for deep people." A listening life is one that resists the easy draw of superficiality and digs past the surface, past the thin veneer to where the deepest truths lie.

# Sacramental Living

*M*y mother moved from Colorado to North Dakota last fall. She had lived and worked in Colorado for over forty years. Making this move allowed Mom to be closer to her sister and her own mother, both in good health, while she herself endured chemotherapy. None of us imagined that her time there would be so short. Mom died just a few months later of complications from pneumonia. Her story ended like so many these days, too quickly, too painfully, another victim of cancer, a tragically familiar sequence of events.

Before cancer invaded her life, Mom had given herself, heart and soul, to the children at the private preschool where she worked. She didn't earn a tremendous salary, nor did she gain any notable professional status. She was an administrative assistant, the first person parents and children met when they walked into school. Every weekday Mom's Hollywood smile and wide-open arms embraced each child as they reluctantly said goodbye to their parents. My mother's hugs were legendary, her voice musical. Her radical commitment to the Denver Broncos dictated her Monday-after-the-game wardrobe. She made coming to school fun.

After her passing, our family decided to have her memorial service in the place that had been the source of her joy and the object of her love. On a summer evening we gathered (family, preschool co-workers, parents, children) in the school's multi-purpose room.

We acknowledged the "Autumn Blaze" maple tree that had been planted in the playground in Mom's memory (red being her favorite color), and we provided a bronze plaque for its base, inscribed with Mom's name and the appropriate descriptor, "Loving Friend of Children." We sang, prayed, and heard stories about the compassionate and enthusiastic ways she loved all those families. I marveled at the joy and gratitude expressed in that service.

What I hadn't expected was how all of those stories, many told to me through tears of parents and kids alike, would provide such clarified insight into the fabric of Mom's life. How she helped a child with learning disabilities transition into school; how she called worried parents in the middle of the day, assuring them that their previously teary child was doing well; how she remembered names of children ten and fifteen years after they had grown and left her. I knew Mom had loved her job, that she poured herself into it with great abandon. But I lived in a different state. I never really got to see her in action.

With each story about my mother, something previously amorphous began to take shape. Flesh and bone was in front of me, testifying to my mother's profound influence upon lives. I hadn't been able to touch that before. What had been unseen and inexperienced became a tangible gift.

I believe the abundance of love my mother had for people was the love of God incarnate. His joy and compassion were made flesh in her, and I encountered it the night of her memorial service. I believe God presents himself through human beings, each one bearing his image. His Word is spoken through his

Body, the Church, of which my mother was, and is, a member.

God's voice and presence often come to us sacramentally; that is, God often speaks to us about invisible, intangible truths via visible, material means. The ultimate and exceptional example of this is the incarnation of Christ, the Word becoming flesh and dwelling among us. Ethereal, unapproachable truth became matter freely accessed. The transcendent and heavenly became earthbound, present and solid, speaking and sleeping, eating, weeping, bleeding, dying.

Jesus made a point of teaching us that the Father would continue to use matter to connect with us. "And he took bread, gave thanks and broke it, and gave it to them, saying, 'This is my body given for you; do this in remembrance of me'" (Luke 22:19).

The sacrament of communion is recognized throughout Christendom, and most Christian traditions use it as a time for self-examination and repentance, an appropriate response to the sacrifice of Christ on our behalf. However, a posture of listening suggests that perhaps God, while eagerly hearing our words of confession and responding with forgiveness, may likewise have something to say *to us* through this sacrament. If a sacrament is the outward and visible sign of an inward and invisible reality, then perhaps we are not the only ones to speak when partaking.

God himself reaches us through the matter of bread and wine if we are attentive to the movement of his Spirit. I am profoundly moved when communion is served in a quiet and reverential way, because it allows me to meditate on that night in the upper room, to become one of the disciples who are first hearing Jesus' shocking prediction. To receive the bread and wine from the Lord himself reminds me, each time, that this is his gift *to me*. The word "Eucharist" means "thanksgiving." Jesus gives me himself each time I take the communion elements, and I hear him say, "This is for *you*." It becomes an intimate encounter with the Lord, mediated by earthly elements of bread and wine.

So, Jesus has profoundly demonstrated that material can speak of the spiritual, and that we can hear the voice of God by paying attention to the tangible means he brings to our attention. A listening life is one that hones the skill of observation, sometimes through the use of metaphor. Long before the last meeting of the disciples in the upper room, Jesus had begun to train them in this skill. "The kingdom of God is like ..." he would begin, and would always fill in the blank with something tangible: a mustard seed, a grain of wheat, a coin. "Look at the flowers of the field," he would say, or "look at the birds of the air." All of creation was good teaching material! Every educator knows that using something tangible (the "object lesson") is a tried and true method of inciting epiphany, that gratifying "aha!" that confirms the truth.

The Psalms provide substantial images that lead us to deeper understanding.

> Blessed is the man
>   who does not walk in the counsel of the wicked
> or stand in the way of sinners
>   or sit in the seat of mockers.
> But his delight is in the law of the LORD,

and on his law he meditates day and night.
He is like a tree planted by streams of water,
    which yields its fruit in season
and whose leaf does not wither.
    Whatever he does prospers.
(*Psalm 1:1-3*)

The image is of a tree whose roots draw nourishment from the water. In the same way, a blessed man or woman draws nourishment from the Lord.

Sacramental truth can come to us from the unexpected, even from something we might consider "secular." God doesn't reside only in places designated as Christian. To suggest that he does should strike us as ludicrous. Yet we easily fall into compartmentalization: Christian music, Christian movies, and Christian books. These can be helpful categories. But in assigning such categories, we need to avoid the implication that God is not present or cannot speak through "non-Christian" media or events as well.

Last summer we traveled throughout Great Britain with twelve university students. On our first day in London, we embarked on our traditional trek to see the changing of the guards at Buckingham Palace. Every time we've done this, we've experienced tremendous crowds, shoving, and too much waiting. The eventual pomp and circumstance itself gets rather long, and in the end, some might say it's over-rated. But it's London—you can't miss it.

So how does one creatively pass the time, standing shoulder to shoulder with other tourists, waiting for the big show? This is what I asked myself. I suppose it was the Holy Spirit who tapped me on the shoulder (or was it someone wanting me to take their picture?) because at some point I was reminded to look. LOOK. Don't just stand around thinking nothing's happening. *What do you see?*

In front of me a wide space led out of the main gates of the palace. This was the place where all the marching in and out would eventually occur. During the waiting time, however, the police let people walk back and forth across that space in front of the palace. So I watched them.

I studied their faces: Pakistani, Chinese, African, Korean, Middle-Eastern, a veritable United Nations parade. Then I listened to the conversations around me in so many different languages. (One of our students reported hearing seven.) And the simple observation came to me, an invisible truth made visible: "Each bears the image of God. And God knows each of their stories." It was rather arresting, this old truth playing out before me, visually reminding me of how deep and wide is the love of God. I've seen the changing of the guards before. But I haven't *heard God* at the changing of the guards before.

Recently I had a delightful chat with my friend, Savannah, a graduate student who works in our office planning events and spiritual growth opportunities for her peers. She and I are separated significantly in age (she could be my daughter), yet we share a fanatical enthusiasm for the popular band, Coldplay. I shared her anticipation: she was going to LA to see them in concert. And with third row seats, I was beyond envious.

As we gushed together about how great this was going to be, we wondered, through our giggles, why epic concerts like this can seem like "religious experiences." Fixed in my memory was our Coldplay experience back in the fall, celebrating with the crowd as the band played one of their most joyful, exuberant tunes while thousands of multicolored tissue-paper butterflies descended upon us. Why did I have tears in my eyes that night? Why did I feel the joy in my heart mounting to the point of bursting?

A Coldplay concert is not what would traditionally be called "sacred." But the thrilling response one has in the presence of excellent music, creatively presented, and enjoyed with thirty thousand people can be compared to a divine encounter, even when presented in a distinctly secular setting. *Why is this?*

I can answer quickly: it *was* a divine encounter. It was an encounter with the joyful, creative, musical, celebratory God that makes himself known in all places, without limitation. Jesus himself said that if his followers didn't praise him, the rocks would cry out. *All* of creation will declare the glory of God, one way or the other. The fall of humanity did not wipe out his image in us or his ability to make his presence known in whatever way he chooses.

Even rock stars, if their work is fine and shared for the betterment of others, can contribute to the great universal paean of praise. My father-in-law, who spent many years as a college president, had a phrase he loved to recite: "Excellence honors God."

There is a universal longing among the followers of Christ—a longing to see him in front of us, to touch him, to know that he is truly with us, that he's not just a mythic figure, that he is a person. The popular declaration that we need a Jesus "with skin on" resonates with a yearning I suspect we all have.

But we find ourselves living in the *meantime*, the time in-between Jesus' earthly life and the time when he will bodily return to us again. In that meantime, giving attention to the things that we can see and touch—the sacramental channels of God's grace and presence—provides a lifeline for us until the day when we, like Thomas, can put our own hands in the hands of Jesus.

# Possessions

When our girls were young, one of the bedtime stories we read to them was a modified version of The Three Bears. The girls enjoyed the tale, but I was captivated by the illustrations. There was something alluring about the artist's depiction of life for the family of three: three plates were set on the table, along with three mugs, three umbrellas in the stand, three pair of shoes by the door, three jackets on hooks. Three of everything. There was precisely enough of everything and nothing extra.

By contrast, my over-consumptive lifestyle troubles me. If an illustrator featured our home in a children's book, she'd show two full sets of dishes plus my wedding china and my grandmother's china; thirty-two mugs in the cupboard; five elusive umbrellas (we can never find them amidst all the stuff in the front hall closet); thirty plus pairs of shoes; and a great gob of jackets in the coat closet. Two drawers in my bedroom are full of the socks that emerge from the dryer without their mates. *Two drawers full of unmatched, random socks.* (We play the Dating Game with these socks now and then to try to get some of them together, yet the number of single socks never diminishes. This means we just keep buying new socks, resulting in a steady rise in our sock population.) Unlike the Three Bears' home, ours has extras of everything.

Scripture instructs us to be wise and generous stewards of the resources given to us. I want to bring my life in line with those principles, whether it means giving away what we no longer use so that someone else can use it, financially sponsoring a child in Brazil, or faithfully tithing and donating our money. The Three Bears show me another biblical principle: that having more than I need is an obstacle to a listening life.

The book's simple drawings resonate with a deep desire in me. I want to be free of what is superfluous, excessive, and unnecessary. St. Ignatius said that we are to be "free of disordered attachments, in order that we may be truly free to find and follow the will of God." The preponderance of our possessions makes it difficult to focus on what is most important. Yet my lifestyle of accumulation continues, filling every available space in my physical and spiritual houses.

My experiences retreating at monastic communities confirm this to me again and again. The first time I stayed at a monastery for spiritual rest and reflection was at a convent in British Columbia. The cell that was my home for those few days was stark and minimally furnished. The walls were of natural wood, and the space was no more than ten feet by ten feet. A small night stand stood next to the twin bed that was covered by a thin, beige bedspread. In the corner a wardrobe housed three melancholy wire hangers. A simple cross of dark wood hung on the wall. No attached bathroom, of course. Even the bears would have found this room sparse.

The profound absence of material items produced a sigh of relief from me; listening would be so much easier here because there were so few things to have to fuss with. No appliances, no extra blankets and pillows in the wardrobe, no complementary bottles of body lotion. No extra anything, because I didn't need any of those things to help me pay attention to God. I had exactly what I needed, and it was enough.

Earlier, I mentioned the Celtic concept of "thin places"—places in the world where the presence of God is curiously more accessible. Of course God is always present no matter where we find ourselves. He is present with me at my favorite bed and breakfast inn as much as he is present at the monastery retreat house. On the contrary, *I* am not always present to *him*. Places like monasteries help us focus and contemplate, in part because we're not overwhelmed by stuff. Thin places are where we can find ourselves as well as God.

Yet much of my daily space and time is "thick," and sadly, it's because I've made my space and time that way. I look around my home, office, car, and see the ways I've thickened my surroundings in ways that do not help me listen. I see the growing stack of envelopes and papers on the counter next to my refrigerator. Two printers take up space on the desk in the study, but neither works. The contents of my over-crowded walk-in closet keep growing. Un-filed papers and folders collect on my desk at the office. (When I ask others to tell me about their thin places, no one ever gives their office desk as an example.)

And life is thick when I listen to the voices of popular culture that work overtime to convince me that *I must have certain items to be a fulfilled, self-actualized person*: a new car, a larger home, fashionable clothes, the latest technological gadget. I can easily justify those purchases, I tell myself, because many other people of faith in my comfy middle class town are giving in, too. When will we have the courage, individually and collectively, to reject the lie that says more is always better?

I'm intrigued by a grassroots movement started by blogger, Dave Bruno. Dave realized that his dependence on possessions was making life more difficult and less meaningful for him. So he made the outrageous decision to whittle his personal possessions down to one hundred items. This must have hit a nerve, because his readers took on the challenge as well. Here's the description from his blog:

> The 100 Thing Challenge is a worldwide grass-roots movement in which people are limiting their material possessions in order to free up physical and mental and spiritual space. People who were once 'stuck in stuff' are empowered to live joyful and thoughtful lives.

Dave's intention is not to be rigid about this, but to prove that life can actually be better *when we have less stuff*. Interestingly, he includes some things on his list that seem unnecessary to me: for example an iPod and a surfboard. So it's not about living primitively, or about denying oneself *all* earthly interests and pleasures. It is, in fact, about denying yourself the stress that comes with managing *too many* possessions, and about making room for more meaning in life when you remove some of your distractions. I can imagine Dave living in his version of the Three Bears' house, happy as a clam with his mug, his plate, his umbrella, and his surfboard.

The curse of an abundance of possessions is not rooted in the possessions themselves, but in what they represent. The things we have are really about *us*. Why do I buy a new purse when I have perfectly good one? Why do I buy a new car when the one I have works fine? Is it because I want to appear a particular way, to have people think one way and not another about me, to feel like I belong to a hip crowd? It is easier to believe the seductive claims of popular culture than it is to answer the penetrating questions of Jesus: "Is not life more than food, and the body more than clothes?" Every day we are tempted to believe that what God has given us—*himself*—is not enough, that we need to go elsewhere.

Jesus knew this temptation out in the desert with the devil nipping at his heels. But he led a listening life, one that encouraged him to hear and believe the truth that God was enough. "Man does not live on bread alone," Jesus shot back at Satan, "but by every word that proceeds from the mouth of God."

When I was a child I sometimes felt I lived in a desert. Although I had everything I needed, my mom and we three kids lived a pretty simple life. It wasn't by choice; we just didn't have much money. Unlike all of my friends, whose families owned their homes, we were *renters*, which in my small mind was the same as admitting, we were *poor*.

Our rented house was a one hundred-year-old, red-brick, one-story cottage. We had no garage, just a driveway made of loose rock and gravel. At the end of the driveway, where a sidewalk might have been, stood an aluminum mail box, fixed to a piece of lumber and cemented into an old fashioned, galvanized milk can. My younger brother and sister and I shared one of the two bedrooms on the main floor above a creepy unfinished basement. When I had the unfortunate task of going down there, I bolted back up the stairs as soon as my task was done, convinced that some dank-smelling monster was on my heels. One summer we discovered that we had bats in our attic, a sinister hoard that emerged at twilight every evening. It was mortifying for a self-conscious nine-year-old.

I coveted the modern homes that my friends lived in, the most enviable were those that had two stories. Any girl who lived in a two-story house had it made, with her own bedroom at the top of a grand, central, white-trimmed staircase. I daydreamed about doing my homework at a white wicker desk that looked out of my high window.

One day in class a boy walked over to my desk, and in a demeaning, snotty tone he said, "Oh, I know you. You're the one that lives in that shack!" *I'd been found out.* I had no idea who this kid was, but it didn't matter. His words pierced my tender renter's psyche. A day or two later I was in my front yard, playing ball with my little sister, and to my horror, I saw the same kid riding toward us on his bike. And this time he wasn't alone. "See!" he shouted to his friend. "I told you she lives in a *shack!*" I was humiliated. I tried to will the attic bats to emerge and move into attack formation. They must have been otherwise occupied.

In my limited nine-year-old sense of identity a house defined my status among my peers. Cool people lived in two-story houses with shutters by the windows and two-car garages. I lived in a shack with bats and a mail box in a milk can, which meant I was at the bottom of my social heap. I lived with this self-imposed stigma until I was fifteen when my family purchased a two-story house. Suddenly I believed all was right with the world.

But all is not right in a world where one's possessions determine one's self-worth. Asaph, one of the Psalmists, wrestles with this dilemma in Psalm 73, complaining about how unfair it is that wicked people seem to increase in wealth and have so few problems. After a good bit of ranting, he emerges with one of the most solid statements of confidence and faith I've heard:

> Whom have I in heaven but you?
> And earth has nothing I desire besides you.
> My flesh and my heart may fail,
> but God is the strength of my heart
> and my portion forever.
> (*Psalm 73:25-26*)

How much stuff do I really need in this world? Well, I do need a *few* things. But I know that when it comes to who I am, and who I'm listening to, *I only need one thing.* "One thing I ask of the Lord," says the writer of Psalm 27, and I repeat it with him regularly, "and this is what I seek: that I may dwell in the house of the Lord all the days of my life, to gaze upon the beauty of the Lord and to seek him in his temple."

# Silence and Stillness

*W*e recently visited good friends in their home on Bainbridge Island, west of Seattle. Linda was one of my roommates in college, and she, Cary, and I sang together in a vocal ensemble. It had been years since we'd seen Linda and her family, so we enjoyed catching up, getting to know each others' kids, and reliving college memories.

Near the end of our visit, Linda called in her dachshund, Harriet, to show us a few tricks. Harriet watched Linda's every move, waited for her command, and obeyed immediately. The most amusing trick was a common one: Linda put a kibble on Harriet's nose, firmly said "Wait," and the dog froze. Not a whimper, not a wiggle. Complete stillness. "Wait," Linda urged the little statue in a quiet but authoritative voice. Many seconds went by. Silence. "Wait," Linda said again, "wait." Then suddenly, in a louder voice, "Good girl!" Harriet whipped her head back and snapped up the kibble, gobbling it down.

Barking comes naturally for small dogs, and they do a lot of it, loudly, for long stretches of time. They also wiggle, run, and whirl around the house, "like a tornado," as my mother used to say when our little black Buffy tore from room to room in my childhood home. That's what little dogs do. Harriet, however, had learned *not* to do the very things that her instincts told her she should do: she learned to be still and quiet.

We thought we were watching a trick, but actually, it was a miracle.

Humans and dachshunds have traits in common. Humans have the urge to move, to dance, to run. We can speak, scream, sing, and hoot. We love activity and noise, like jumping up and down and screaming with seventy thousand other fans when our team scores. We thrill to the throbbing pulse of our favorite rock band in concert. We're elated to raise hands and voices together when we worship. This is what we do and enjoy doing. Yet although every jittery nerve and muscle in our bodies resists, we need silence and stillness as well.

"This is what the Sovereign LORD, the Holy One of Israel, says: 'In repentance and rest is your salvation, in quietness and trust is your strength,'" writes Isaiah in his thirtieth chapter, ending with the chilling phrase, "but you would have none of it."

Repentance. Rest. Quietness. Trust. Scripture is clear that these are at the root of salvation and strength. But self-reliance, hyper-activity, noise, and autonomy come more easily to us.

Jesus regularly made the choice to leave the noise and activity of ministry for a time and go to a place of stillness and silence with his Heavenly Father. Why did he do this when there were fifty more people to heal, another thousand or so to feed, and all of those Pharisees he needed to put in their places? Jesus knew the deep reward that comes from doing nothing, from being still and listening to the voice that would remind him that he was the beloved Son of God. This was the source of his strength. This was what made it possible for him to re-enter the crowds with mercy, compassion, and stamina.

The point of being silent without activity is that it teaches us to release control of our lives. It is similar to the charge that every parent receives at the moment of a child's birth. Not when that child is eighteen or twenty-one, but when they're one hour old. There's a profound holiness to that kind of realization, that this child is mine, yet not mine. With each passing year, they belong more to the world and to God and less to parents. The same is true of our lives: we are not our own. Then why do we, in our chaotic frenzy, pretend otherwise?

In silence and stillness we have the opportunity, as Isaiah suggests, to repent: to turn from our self-centered ways and face God-ward again; to rest: to breathe the sigh of relief that comes from giving God full oversight of our lives; to be quiet: to turn down the external volume so we might listen to the voice of God that is heard in the "sound of sheer silence" (1 Kings 19); and to trust: to once again acknowledge that we are not in charge of the world, at large or at small.

Søren Kierkegaard, the great Danish Christian philosopher wrote an insightful reflection on Jesus' exhortation to "seek first the kingdom of God and his righteousness" in his *Spiritual Writings*:

> What kind of striving is it of which it can be said that it seeks or desires the kingdom of God? Ought I to get a position corresponding to my abilities and powers in order to bring this about? No, you are first to seek the kingdom of God. Ought I, then, to give all my fortune to the poor? No, you are first

to seek the kingdom of God. But does this, then, mean that, in a sense, there is nothing for me to do? Quite right, there is, in a sense, *nothing*. In the very deepest sense, you are to make yourself nothing, to become nothing before God, and learn to keep silent. And in this silence you begin to seek what must come first: the kingdom of God.

Years ago I was part of a group that planned contemplative prayer retreats for women. Our purpose was to give busy women the opportunity to stop their frantic lives and be quiet with God for a day. One of the members of this planning group owned a beautiful, spacious home that she volunteered for our use. Another was a fabulous cook. Another specialized in composing materials to guide us during retreats. Each of us contributed toward the goal of a still, quiet day.

On a rainy Pacific Northwest Saturday morning, our guests arrived to the aroma of freshly brewed coffee and berry muffins just out of the oven. We distributed the materials for the day, including a printed guide for prayer and a spiral-bound blank journal. After filling our coffee mugs, the twenty-five or thirty of us eventually made our way to the large family room. Settled in overstuffed couches, large pillows on the floor, and a fire blazing in the fireplace, the process of de-stressing had begun.

I've had a pretty snarky attitude about retreats for some time. But I have my reasons. Many times I've come home from a retreat more tired than refreshed. Too many retreats are crammed with activity and socializing, lessons and talks about how to be a better Christian woman. I think these activities have their place, but "retreat" traditionally meant to remove ourselves from activity and productivity. We retreat by spending an hour, or a day, or more with God without the distraction of activity, entertainment, and the endless demands of life. That model best mirrors the pattern we see in the life of Jesus.

And it's the image we kept in mind when planning our contemplative retreats. We designated the bulk of the day as silent, with each of us in our own corner or nook. We encouraged the women to be still and listen for whatever God had for them. We suggested scripture reading and journal writing as listening tools. But mostly, we urged them to abandon their ongoing compulsions to be productive, and to rest in the presence of God. Those hours of stillness and silence became, ironically, some of the most productive hours of our week.

At lunch each day, we broke our silence and enjoyed homemade soup and hearty bread together. We shared stories as we ate, but not at the frenetic pace that social settings often encourage. Silence had taken the edge off of our voices. We didn't have to hurry; we had plenty of time to listen to each other. Our conversations were full of substance rather than the trivial. It was a feast for our souls and bodies.

After lunch we again dispersed for silent time, which became easier to settle into. As we gathered a last time at the end of the day, we felt at peace with God and with each other ... and perhaps even with ourselves, ready to re-enter a busy world that needs the peace of God.

The author of Psalm 131 wrote:

> My heart is not proud, LORD,
>    my eyes are not haughty;
> I do not concern myself with great matters
>    or things too wonderful for me.
> But I have calmed and quieted myself,
>    I am like a weaned child with its mother;
>    like a weaned child I am content.

The short Psalm ends with this exhortation:

> Israel, put your hope in the LORD
>    both now and forevermore.

Silence sets us straight. Silence leads to the contentment of a weaned child who no longer grasps for its mother but is happy to simply sit with her. Silence trains our ears to hear the words that God speaks all the time but which are inaudible in the cacophony of life. Silence leads us to say with the Psalmist, "My soul finds rest in God alone," (Psalm 62:1).

# Ancient Voices

Cary and I had just finished clearing away the dishes after dinner when he said, "I realized today that the number of years we've been at the university is the same number of years we have until we retire." That number is fourteen.

Heaviness settled on my shoulders. I told him that sometimes I question whether I'll be able to maintain the energy to help college students. He, in turn, commented on how he feels old when he's around the newer, "cooler" faculty members, and he wonders how long his teaching will seem relevant to his students.

I balanced that bleakness by remembering something one of our guest speakers said in a recent chapel service. Gordon MacDonald, a well-known writer, seasoned pastor, and passionate leader is well into his seventies. He told the audience of almost one thousand people that he is settling into his calling for this last season of his life: "I'm devoting my time to being a spiritual father to young adults."

This is both a correction and a reminder to me. It corrects my fears about my future role in the lives of college students. They will always need spiritual guides and the voices of faithful mentors who are older and wiser. Such sage voices from my past speak regularly to me: Roy and Ruth, my youth pastor and wife; Rahime, my high school discipleship group leader; Vicki, my college small group leader; Margaret, my first spiritual director. Each spoke a truth that at the time I wasn't mature enough to discover myself. The guiding voices in my life coaxed me to follow them as they followed Christ, one step at a time. They listened to God, and they taught me how to listen, too.

Others mentors are voices from a more distant past: Patrick, Benedict, Teresa, to name a few. I've not met them and won't because they're dead. Some of the most influential voices that have coached me in my journey of faith lived many centuries ago in cities and countrysides far from my home in northwest Arkansas. Still, their voices speak from the printed page, and I feel that they know me. In their voices, I hear the voice of God.

I was introduced to the world of ancient devotional writers during my senior year in college when I impulsively registered for an independent study course on "Classic Devotional Material." In hindsight, I recognize that I had no clue what I was in for. Up to that point, "devotional material" had only applied to daily readings in various "quiet time" guides. From the start, my professor threw around names like John of the Cross and Pascal like they were his good buddies, blowing my narrow understanding to bits. I sat, dumbfounded and embarrassed, swimming in waters that were too deep for me.

My professor was kind and did not give up on me. Soon enough he introduced me to an ancient voice that resonated with me: Thomas à Kempis, writer of the classic work, *The Imitation of Christ*. I still have my original copy. The many passages underlined in red tell me that Thomas spoke encouraging and convicting truths to me. "This most of all hinders heavenly consolation, that you are slow in turning to prayer. For before you earnestly ask of Me, you seek other comforts, and refresh yourself in outward things." In the margin, written in the same red ink, is the comment, "ME."

Brother à Kempis had the depth of vision to know that the spiritual battles of the sixteenth century would remain for centuries to come. Outward things continue in their devious plot to distract us from that which brings heavenly consolation. I needed to hear this from as many angles as possible, over and over, reminding me to "seek first the kingdom of God" rather than the kingdoms of this transient world.

In my thirties, I discovered another ancient voice, a woman's. Teresa of Ávila lived in the same century as à Kempis, but wrote from a convent in Spain. She is widely recognized as a great contemplative soul and a woman of deep prayer and devotion. In her autobiography, she said:

> It is painful to me that our confidence in God is so scanty, and our self-love so strong, such that any anxiety about our necessities should disturb us. But so it is, for when our spiritual progress is so slight, a mere nothing will give us as much trouble as great and important matters will give to others.

In other words, excessive self-love and anxiety feed off of each other. This deeply perceptive, prayerful woman spoke contemporary truth from an ancient vantage. In my late thirties self-focus became a monkey on my back, but more from necessity than vanity. With two children needing continual attention, a significant crisis at work that gave me stomach aches, and a husband sparring with a chronic disease, it was easy to become fixated on my own troubles. There were days when the cloak of fretfulness and fear wrapped itself so tightly around my shoulders that I felt paralyzed and could hardly breathe. I remember anxiety so acute I couldn't sit in a drive-through car wash without profound claustrophobia, as if the soap-squirting, auto-buffing monster might squeeze me into non-existence.

I realized I needed to break free of the vortex of self-absorption and anxiety, the enemies that were conspiring to draw me from the love of God and the exhilaration of life. It was time to get some help. I arranged to see a counselor who, in time, explained that my own physiology played a role in my acute anxiety. Sometime later, the combination of a God-fearing counselor, a prescription for medication, and the healing power of God helped set me right again.

Teresa was right. When we turn in upon ourselves too intensely, it can draw us away from the peace of God, and anxiety and fear result.

Of all the wise voices of the past that I've listened to, I feel the most affection for Thomas Kelly. He wasn't an ancient saint; his *Testament of Devotion* was published in 1941. Although a short book, it has loomed large in my life for many years. Kelly was a Quaker, a tradition that has always appealed to me because of its insistence on listening and silence as essential elements of the centered Christian life.

After re-reading it many times, Kelly's book has also suffered from my repeated underlining and annotations. Here's a line from *A Testament of Devotion* I always want to re-underline: "holy and listening and alert obedience remains as the core and kernel of a God-intoxicated life." It's a compelling description of the life I desire. This vision of the God-intoxicated life may emerge from words printed on a page, but as I read them I imagine Kelly's voice proclaiming them with conviction. His voice speaks, decades later, urging me to settle for nothing less.

Kelly continues, later in *A Testament of Devotion*:

> There is a divine Abyss within us all, a holy Infinite Center, a Heart, a Life who speaks in us and through us to the world. We have all heard this holy Whisper at times. At times we have followed the Whisper, and amazing equilibrium of life, amazing effectiveness of living set in. But too many of us have heeded the voice only at times. Only at times have we submitted to His holy guidance. We have not counted this Holy Thing within us to be the most precious thing in the world. We have not surrendered all else, to attend to it alone.

The owners of these ancient voices have been my soul friends and my "soul food" especially when a kindred spirit isn't available in the flesh. Changing jobs, uprooting and moving to a new state or country, and even our own emotional state can be the cause of real loneliness and a feeling that soul friends are few and far between. The state of our souls suffers because of our penchant to uproot and change with dizzying frequency. When our family moved from Washington to Arkansas, the provision of a new ministry and a new community thrilled me. But I left behind some dear soul friends in the process. It took many months to form new relationships in Arkansas, and many more before they could begin to touch the depth of relationship I had with my friends in Washington. In those months of waiting for friendships to grow, I found spiritual friendships through the writing of some of the great saints of old. Sure, it's not the same as hearing the voice of a friend or sitting in their presence. But those ancient voices were helpful substitutes. I needed words of wisdom, and they provided that for me when there were no earthly soul friends in sight.

Hebrews 11 displays a great list of faithful voices of the ancient people of God: Abel, Noah, Abraham, Sarah, Isaac, Jacob, Joseph, Moses, and Rahab. These represent the "great cloud of witnesses" that surrounds us, declares the writer of Hebrews. If I listen to their voices I will encounter the faithfulness and goodness of God. These ancient voices, in addition to those who have lived since, provide necessary correction or re-orientation when I overreact to the challenges of life.

When I hear newscasters predict economic disaster and am tempted to fear, I turn my ears to Moses who reminds me that the Lord gave the Israelites bread, meat, and water in the desert. When I am tempted to try to impress others by my cleverness or wit, I listen to St. Benedict as he taught his monastic brothers the way of humility: "The wise man is known by the fewness of his words." When I hear about the persecution of faithful Christians, I listen to Dietrich Bonhoeffer, martyred for his faith, who reminds me that suffering is often a part of discipleship and a cross I should be prepared to bear.

The great saints, from Ignatius to Martin Luther to Madame Guyon to Hannah Whitall Smith, sing out with uncanny clarity and wisdom for our modern world. They are voices of faith who "still [speak], even though [they are] dead" (Hebrews 11:4), members of the great cloud of witnesses whose testimonies guide us into attentive, listening lives.

# When Listening is a Gift

Today I had lunch with Laura, a former student who has returned to our quaint town after three years of living and working in southern California. We sat together in our local café, drinking iced orange spice tea, munching toasted sandwiches, and marveling at the differences between high-energy West Coast life and the sleepy charm of Siloam Springs. As our conversation turned to our professional lives, I was jolted from the café's comfort to a much larger and more ominous world: Laura is the executive director of a Christian organization that helps restore women in India who have been victims of sexual trafficking.

In our ninety minutes together we barely scratched the surface of what she has learned through this work, and how she has seen God do miracles in India. She told me about the Indian leper colonies she has seen and about the sewing centers her organization creates for women who are victims of the sex trade. She told me about pastors in India who live selflessly in the meanest of conditions, caring for multiple foster children. My eyes teared-up as she related these stories. But she laughed and said, "I sometimes don't tell people what I do because they always act amazed, as if it's a big deal. But really, my part is small." I ended up laughing with her because I could never do what she does. It *is* a big deal.

Having worked in college ministry for fourteen years, I've heard many remarkable stories. This generation's university students do a lot of *big* things. We watch our students grow during the four years they're with us. Then in May of their senior year we watch them walk across the commencement stage, receive their diplomas, and keep right on walking, determined to do something helpful in this weary world.

Laura and I also talked about our mutual friend, Hannah. Throughout her undergraduate and graduate degrees at our university, Hannah and I met almost weekly to listen to God's voice in her life. Hannah has a lightning-quick mind, a deeply compassionate heart, and an insatiable appetite for cross-cultural engagement. Most recently, Hannah has been working with a relief agency in Afghanistan. As Laura and I spoke fondly about our common friend, our incredulity was mutual: *what young woman would have the guts to serve needy people in the midst of a war zone?* Laura smiled and shook her head at Hannah's bravery.

Laura doesn't realize it, but she and Hannah are cut from the same cloth. I, on the other hand, am painfully aware that I am cut from something different, and the contrast has concerned me for years. While my former students are out there doing selfless, compassionate, often dangerous things in the name of Jesus, I am chatting with a student in my comfortable office, drinking hot tea. While these passionate young Christians give up the American dream for the sake of the "least of these" that Christ speaks of, I am quietly praying with a circle of my colleagues. Laura's and Hannah's work often involves exposure to disease, living great distance from loved ones, and (heaven forbid) a lack of air conditioning. My work involves creative projects, warm relationships, stimulating discussions ... and Starbuck's coffee. People like Laura and Hannah are cut from something like Pendleton wool: sturdy, useful, tough, and beautiful. I feel like a crocheted doily.

This internal battle has troubled me for much of my adult life, repeatedly making me ask if I'm truly following the way of the cross. Much of what I do with students and colleagues is listen to them and pray with them, with the goal of discerning God's direction for their lives. That doesn't seem very brave or world-changing. I ask them questions, like "So where do you see God in this?" or, "What do you think God wants you to do, see, feel, or think?" It's what I did with Hannah all of those years; and now she's in Afghanistan. Perhaps my doily-role, listening and watching with Hannah, has helped her become the Pendleton wool woman that God is calling her to be.

What I'm learning is that while listening to another person may seem passive and unadventurous, it can be a holy calling, and a great gift we can give one another. In our texting and emailing world, we seldom find opportunities to share, at length, our own story with someone who will listen with the open ears of Jesus. I grieve over the physical poverty that exists in our world, and do what I can, in my own small ways, to help relieve that suffering. But I'm also aware of *spiritual* poverty, the desperate need we each have to hear a word from the One who loves us beyond all comprehension. Attentive, compassionate listening can be a remarkably healing channel of love.

Intentional listening was an integral part of life for ancient Christians living in the British Isles. In their monastic communities, it was essential that each member have an *anamchara*, Gaelic for "soul friend."

This was a fellow member of the community who was often older and wiser, who served as confessor and guide in the walk of faith. The *anamchara* was there to help discern where God was at work and to provide an opportunity for confession and forgiveness. It seems like these kinds of relationships would be easy to come by in our modern world, connected as we are by devices that give us instant access to each other. But I fear the reverse is true.

Listening is a gift when niggling questions keep us up at night. My friend Kim has been helping me listen to God about the decisions I need to make about the care of my invalid father, who is physically distant from me. I am having a very difficult time discerning the call of God in this matter. Kim listens to me every week as I chew on the latest details of the situation and my internal struggles. She listens patiently as I babble on. She asks me great questions that help me think through this carefully. The three of us (Kim, God, and I) are slogging our way through. The process is invaluable to me, for I can't trust myself and my limited perspective in a situation that pulls me in different directions.

Sharing life with a listener is also helpful when our faith seems dead altogether, when God seems absent, when the Scriptures taste like cardboard in our mouths. This is a common experience for all Christians, regardless of how "together" our spiritual lives may appear. The world is not as God intended. Pain and injustice makes it harder to believe that God is gracious, compassionate, slow to anger, and abounding in loving kindness. How does a young wife hang on to faith when she receives the call about her husband's sudden death? How can a young man profess a lively faith in a Heavenly Father when his earthly father is cruel and abusive? Why does a faithful Christian have to wait for months for employment when the Scripture says that God's plans for her are to "prosper and not to harm" (Jeremiah 29:11)?

Each of us has spiritual knots that need untying, some more serious than others. In such times, a "soul friend," a listener, is a way for God to bring us back to a place of peace and stability. When I listen to someone struggling I become aware of the presence of God, and I want the one sharing with me to realize that presence. The act of slowing, of focusing, of looking the speaker in the eye, conveys the compassion of God, and there is an awareness of the Holy in the room. Concrete answers may or may not come. But a deeper sense of connection with God is always the result, and with it the conviction of Julian of Norwich, that whether here on earth, or at a later date in eternity, "all will be well, and all manner of thing will be well."

Sometimes a more formal arrangement of spiritual direction—discerning the shape and meaning of the Spirit's workings in one's life—is what we need. It is formal in the sense of a recurring meeting time, where one person serves as the director and the other as directee. The director enters into this relationship with the intention of serving as an attentive, listening presence to the one who has requested it.

I completed a training program for certification as a spiritual director. But formal training is not essential to be effective in a ministry of listening and discernment. The Catholic tradition has included this kind of relationship in the life of their church for hundreds of years. In addition to the ancient Celtic Christians, we can access historical models such as John Wesley, whose "bands and classes" of the eighteenth century met regularly to discuss the state of their souls.

Over many months I met regularly with a small group of female colleagues for what we called a "discernment group." We were growing and faithful believers, but we didn't fain perfection. I wasn't interested in hosting a group where we only shared the happy stories. We needed honest disclosure about the questions we were confronting in our lives, questions which had become tangled and mangled. We wanted to help each other discern how God was speaking into all of that.

We met during our lunch hour. I always lit a candle to remind us that the Holy Spirit of God himself was there with us. We then had a short time of silence to help us move into a receptive listening mode. One of us came prepared to be the presenter who had freedom to speak of her need for God's wisdom. We shared our concerns about our families, frustrations with God, and professional issues. While one of us spoke, those listening stayed true to a commitment to remain silent and listening. The speaker had freedom from interruption and unsolicited advice. After about ten minutes, she stopped, and we returned to a prayerful silence, where we each asked for the Spirit's help, resisting the temptation to rush in with our own explanations of experience and advice.

The temptation to give advice is hard to resist. I remember in high school when my best friend Joanna called to tell me that a boy had invited her to the high school homecoming dance (a big deal in those turbulent teenage days). But the boy who asked wasn't the boy she was hoping for. I brazenly said, "Well here's all you need to do about that." With her characteristic grace and directness, Joanna said, "Tracy, I wasn't asking you for advice." I had completely missed what she wanted: to be heard, for me to listen!

"You cannot do everything. But what you can do, you must do," says U2's Bono. I will pray and support courageous people like Laura and Hannah as they work to defeat poverty, disease, and human trafficking. And I will keep wearing my silver bracelet, engraved with the word *anamchara*, "soul friend," reminding me to be faithful to my calling in a world of spiritual poverty: I will listen.

# Compassion

The sign read, "Please wear these socks for walking the labyrinth." Beneath it, someone had left a large plastic storage box full of pristine, fluffy white socks. Whatever I had expected to experience by walking this prayer labyrinth, it was not the simple pleasure of putting on comfortable virgin socks.

But the sign made sense. The sprawling canvas labyrinth in the great cathedral was worth protecting from the scuffs that shoes would leave. I removed my sandals and put on the socks for the prayer walk.

I took note of other ways the staff at the Washington National Cathedral tried to make this a meaningful experience. On a small table, a stack of neon green leaflets explained the labyrinth: "The earliest known Christian labyrinth is located on the wall of a church in Algeria," and, "the labyrinth in the floor of the nave at Chartres Cathedral in France is the most well-known of the medieval designs." The labyrinth is a tool to help people become aware of the presence of God. There was also a pleasant woman sitting at the labyrinth entrance, the *Book of Common Prayer* open on her lap, a name tag pinned to her blouse. She looked up and beamed warmly whenever anyone entered the labyrinth. Meanwhile, near the front of the church, a slight woman played softly on a harp. It was as if we'd been invited to a grand party and the hostess had attended to every detail.

This wasn't my first time to pray through a labyrinth. I'd visited an outdoor labyrinth at the St. Scholastica monastery, just a couple of hours from my Arkansas home. I spent part of an afternoon walking leisurely on its rock-lined path. I repeated the ancient Jesus Prayer: "Lord Jesus Christ, Son of God, have mercy on me," letting the labyrinth guide me, savoring the silence among the monastery woods.

But my experience at the National Cathedral was markedly different. I was not alone. Some of my fellow walkers were new acquaintances I made at the writing workshop that week at the Cathedral College of Preachers. And there were others on the path who were strangers to me. We each waited for our turn, quietly entering the labyrinth one by one.

The time came for me, wearing socks like everyone else, to enter. I instinctively began praying the Jesus Prayer again, but my head and heart were battling, as I silently questioned whether this experience would amount to anything. I knew that the presence of others easily distracts me. I knew I would wonder about the spiritual orientation of my fellow walkers. Are they here because they want more of God? Or are they just going through the motions? Maybe they are of a completely different faith than I, since the labyrinth is a tool of prayer in non-Christian religions as well. I knew of course that the unseen motives of another person's heart were God's business, not mine. But I was distracted nonetheless.

I walked on, one slow step after the other, "Lord Jesus Christ, Son of God, have mercy on me, a sinner." I bowed my head and kept to the path before me, trying to stay focused and not distracted by others. I soon learned this was futile, as the narrowness of the lanes forced me to pay attention to those ahead of and behind me. I had to take care not to drift into oncoming traffic and inadvertently cause an embarrassing collision.

The labyrinth carried us in a circular motion, switching back now and then, the path paralleling itself over and over. This meant that with every switch back I would re-encounter the same pairs of feet on the path next to me. Most often I noticed the feet of those I didn't know. A young father walked with his two children, one a carefree girl of maybe seven, and her younger brother who seemed unaware that this was supposed to be a quiet activity. *Why must he jingle that change in his pocket with every step? Lord Jesus Christ, have mercy on me, a sinner.* Someone else walked by me, wearing funky striped socks. The feet of an elderly woman passed me. The next pair had a familiar shape: college-student feet. I felt a surge of affection for that pair.

I recognized the feet of my fellow workshop attendees, the petite feet of my new friend Marta, the casual khaki slacks of Jim, a clergyman from St. Louis. I added these people to my prayers: *Lord Jesus Christ, Son of God, have mercy on Marta ... have mercy on Jim.* I noticed the feet of those whom I had learned, through our time in the writing group, were part of the gay community. I prayed the Jesus Prayer for them and for me; I'd learned to love them that week even though we think differently on some important matters.

Actually, I thought differently than most of the people in my writing group. It became clear, very early in our week together, that I was the token "evangelical" in the group. I have mixed feeling about that label because its meaning gets convoluted. I consider myself quite moderate when it comes to politics; conservative when it comes to the authority of scripture. As I listened to my fellow participants share their writing that week, it became clear to me that I was the odd woman out.

I knew before arriving that this would likely be the case, so with the Psalmist, I asked the Lord to "place a guard over my mouth," trusting God to remind me regularly that I did not need to make brilliant comments. I needed to listen to the stories of these fellow Christians, even though we looked at life and faith through different lenses.

I listened as they shared their written reflections. These included twists and turns that were theologically troubling to me. Some of the essays offered took wild liberties with the biblical text, making me squirm in my seat. Certain views of God ruffled my evangelical sensibilities. I heard fluid, amorphous perspectives on our eternal destination that made me uncomfortable. I silently prayed for help and fidgeted with my pen as they shared their thoughts and ideas. I wanted desperately to be able to disagree respectfully with them yet simultaneously embrace them as my brothers and sisters.

Our group's writing mentor happened to know me well enough to perceive my silent struggle and gave me a side-long whisper later that week. "How're you doing?" she asked with a knowing look. It felt good to have someone acknowledge the dissonance I was feeling.

A few years ago our oldest daughter, Kelsey, and I were in Northern Ireland on a mission trip. One afternoon our group visited an outdoor maze entirely created out of sculpted shrubbery on the grounds of a castle in a quaint village. As Kelsey and I ran into one tall leafy wall of shrubbery after another, our frustration increased. The whole experience made us feel trapped, stupid, and helpless, only made worse by the periodic shouts of "I'm out!" by our friends who had conquered the task.

That Irish maze served as a metaphor for my experience in the DC writing group. So much about the workshop was beautiful: the people, the setting, the subject matter. And yet over and over I found myself running into walls and feeling trapped. It wasn't that I resented my own convictions; it was, rather, my apparent inability to walk the maze of faith with these who were so vocal about following a different route. Surely we could walk this path together!

And now here we were on a labyrinth of prayer in a holy place. We were strangers, friends, seekers, each needing the mercy of God.

I continued with the Jesus Prayer. The music of the harp reminded me that slowness is good for the soul. The soaring buttresses of the cathedral gave me plenty of space to breathe my prayers. And when I finally arrived at the center of the labyrinth, I didn't feel claustrophobic or stupid. I sat down on the small circular space where walkers could stop for quiet prayer and meditation, ready to listen for what God wanted me to hear.

The Jesus Prayer and the labyrinth collaborated to bring me to both a literal and a spiritual center, a contemplative place of experiencing the love of God. This is, in fact, how a labyrinth is supposed to work: as we walk slowly and prayerfully toward its center, we gradually release all concerns and preoccupations with ourselves, coming, finally, to the center space where we realize, as the Psalmist says, that "earth has nothing I desire besides you" (Psalm 73:25).

I sat in the center, receiving God's love for me in a way that was completely unhurried, watching those young and old, gay and straight, liberal and conservative, believing and seeking feet. Suddenly I felt a wave of consolation: it was good to be walking this path with my new friends. It was good that I wasn't walking this labyrinth alone. God had put me on that twisting path with everyone else, each of us with mixed up motives and plenty to learn.

I rose from the center of the labyrinth to begin the journey out, symbolizing "going out into the world." Bumping into others, stepping outside of my lane and then back in again, seeing Marta's feet go by once more, listening to the harp, I was filled with humble gratitude for the mercy that Jesus did indeed give. Listening, I knew he was asking *me* to give mercy as well.

I really couldn't know for sure where my fellow walkers were on their journey of faith (a "labyrinth path" of life, as it were). But I could be content in knowing that by walking the labyrinth, they, we, were all facing God. It would seem that in facing God, the only way to walk is God-ward, and that's a good thing. It can only get better from there.

# *Journeying*

*E*very day we have opportunities to listen to God. Unforeseen gifts and lessons await those who have the patience to recognize and accept them. Even in the dead of winter, if we are still, quiet, observant, and open to the unexpected paths laid out before us, God will bless us with new growth and warm encounters with the resurrection life.

Day One

I'm sitting in the Newark Airport, waiting for time to pass. Outside the concourse window the New York City skyline, now lit up by the afternoon sun, provides a striking backdrop for the jumbo jets parading back and forth on the tarmac. Cary is grading theology papers next to me. We have a seven-hour layover before we board our overnight flight to Belfast; he should get a lot of grading done.

I'm eager to be in Ireland again, though this will be my first visit in winter. I'm looking forward to seeing Belfast at Christmas, although I know this means short, dark days. The early Celtic Christians in Ireland knew how to watch for God while journeying. As they traveled, their objective was to seek the "place of their resurrection." On this trip I am asking myself and God to help me spot such places. *Where will I see evidence of new life, in myself or in others?*

After we arrived in Newark, we walked to a stairway that led us down to the shuttle bus for the international concourse. I flashed back to another time I connected through Newark on my way to a conference on the East Coast. It was a travel experience that hadn't been entirely pleasant. My connection time was too short; I had too much to carry; it was beastly hot; and I was stressed about the presentation I would make at the conference. I ran down one of those staircases, sweating, worried I was going in the wrong direction, with no time to get lost.

At the bottom of the stairs at a check-in desk, three female employees (two of them African American, one Caucasian) were laughing hysterically. They seemed oblivious to my presence, so I curtly interrupted their levity and asked, "Is this where I catch the shuttle bus?" "That's right!" one of them said, smiling. "OK, what do I need to do?" I asked impatiently. The plump, grinning black woman looked at me, eyes twinkling, and said, "Girl, you gotta dance."

That was not the response I expected or wanted. "You're serious," I said. "Yep!" she said, and waited. I stared back at her in disbelief. Then, gathering the few particles of positive energy I had in my reserves, I took a deep breath and busted out my best walk-like-an-Egyptian dance. The three women erupted again, cackling with laughter, "You go, girl! Get on that bus!" The work those women do, day after day, cannot be terribly gratifying. But on that day, they showed me how to invite a moment of resurrection life into my otherwise dreadful day.

Now we're flying over the Atlantic, finally, after a two-hour delay sitting on the tarmac in Newark. I've awoken from a cat nap to a dark cabin. Cary is snoozing along with the majority of the other passengers. We've been in the air for four hours, so out my window I see the first hints of sunrise changing the colors of the sky. A bright sliver of moon hovers over a quilt of clouds. The air is so clear that the moon's entire spherical shape is visible, a marble hanging in the sky. Above it shines Jupiter, star-like and brilliant. I say a prayer of thanks and close my eyes again.

Day Two

Our taxi drove us through the Belfast I had anticipated; twinkling lights festooned the city center, snow draped the dormers of houses in Christmas-card neighborhoods. We've arrived at Lakeside Manor, our university's home away from home. This is our first visit to Lakeside. We step through the door of the one hundred-year-old manor house and receive a warm welcome from our friends and colleagues from John Brown University. Then we haul our bags up the three narrow flights of stairs to our room to quickly freshen up. We've made it just in time to attend a banquet celebrating the students' successful completion of their semester of Irish studies. In a few days they'll return to the United States, changed forever by their experience here.

The banquet takes place at a nearby hotel. I feel another twinge of excitement seeing the students dressed in their Christmas best, taking pictures together by the decorated trees in the hotel. We gradually make our way to the banquet room where a striking young woman is playing the Celtic harp. Cary and I choose seats between Sarah and Eric, a young American couple who work at Lakeside, and John, our American friend who teaches in our Irish studies program while pursuing his doctoral degree at Queen's University in Belfast. I'm delighted to see traditional Christmas crackers—gaily wrapped paper tubes that crack and pop when pulled open—sitting on our dinner plates. Sarah takes one end, and I take the other, and POP, her cracker opens, revealing a tissue paper crown (promptly donned) and a tiny plastic angel. The rest of us follow suit, and soon there are paper crowns on all heads around the table. I remember the Christmas dinner scene in the movie "Shadowlands" and decide that if C. S. Lewis can wear a silly Christmas crown, so can I.

The celebrative air is contagious. There is delectable food: carrot and cinnamon crème soup, warm grainy rolls, ham, turkey, stuffing, and two different kinds of potatoes, followed by "Christmas pudding"—a dense, fig cake with sauce, surely the same "figgy pudding" that the English carol "We Wish You a Merry Christmas" refers to. We do some group carol singing of our own, accompanied by the harp. As I survey the scene, I see the faces of friends we've made through our visits to Ireland over the last ten years. Gratitude fills my heart.

<u>Day Three</u>

We're freezing. Lakeside Manor is full of vintage British charm, with its varying roof lines, grand staircase, bold floral carpet, and miniature sleeping rooms. But the recent snowfall and dropping temperatures have created a chill in this old building. I've begun doubling up on socks and wearing layers of clothing whether they go together or not. A "slashing hot cup of tea" (as our Irish friend Bill calls it) is the remedy of choice.

At ten o'clock in the morning, Hadden Wilson arrives at Lakeside to take Cary and me to Killyleagh, the village our mission team will be serving this summer. Hadden wears many hats for JBU here "on the ground" in Northern Ireland. He has the experience and heart of a pastor, the intellect of a scholar, and the energy of a twenty-year old. Hadden is one of my favorite people, and I'm delighted at the prospect of a forty-five-minute ride with him to Killyleagh.

We make the most of our time as we ride through the snow dusted countryside. Our mission to Ireland is important to Hadden as well, and he has many thoughts to share as he drives.

Killyleagh proves to be an endearing seaside Irish village of small homes and quaint shops, with a castle in the center of town. At a tiny coffee shop about one hundred paces from the castle, we meet with Nicola McWhirter to discuss our summer plans. Nicola is a bright and affable young woman who has been working with Youth for Christ in Killyleagh for three years. Over coffee and pastries, Nicola talks to us about the youth in the village, their general boredom that often leads to drugs and alcohol, and how we might reach them during our summer visit. She tells us about the churches in town and how we can partner with them in ministry. I tell her that we have no desire to be the presumptuous Americans, the sole possessors of effective ministry "riding in on white horses." We simply want to offer ourselves as the hands and feet of Christ. We rely on her wisdom regarding the particular shape that might take.

I feel good about our meeting, impressed at Nicola's commitment to the youth of Killyleagh, and grateful to have her on our side. I know that in the coming months, some of the folks we see in the village, doing their daily business, will become our friends. We'll worship with them in their churches, teach, and sing and play with their children.

Day Four

I am disappointed. I got ready for church this morning, had my coat and gloves on, and then suddenly felt queasy, dizzy, and weak. It was enough to convince Cary to go on with the group to church without me. I kept my winter coat on in defense against the chill in the house. I lay down on the couch in the family room and napped.

Now I'm back upstairs in our room, feeling much better, sitting on the floor with my feet propped on the radiator, and making the most of some private time with God while I wait for the group to return.

Another plan thwarted, this time by the weather. Cary and I were to drive to Downpatrick to visit some cottages we hope to house our mission team in this summer. The temperatures plummeted overnight, and when Cary turned the key in the car we were to use, there was no response. So we called the cottage owners, rescheduled for later in the week, and sat down for a hot cup of tea.

This afternoon our friend John is accompanying us on a city bus ride to Queen's University. There is a new reading room in the Queen's library that I am eager to see. It is dedicated to C. S. Lewis. Lewis grew up not far from here; his mother was a Queen's graduate.

Since John is a doctoral student at Queen's, he's our ticket in.

One of Northern Ireland's great preachers and scholars, Derick Bingham, played a significant role in the creation of the room. Derick, like Hadden, has been a good friend to our university. As the plans for the room were first coming together, Derick was especially excited about new developments. "Walden Media has agreed to allow the wardrobe door that was used in the filming of 'The Lion, The Witch, and The Wardrobe' to reside in the Lewis room!" he said as we chatted in Belfast a few years ago. Derick died of leukemia almost a year ago, and Belfast isn't quite right without him. But now seeing the wardrobe door and the grand portrait of Aslan colorfully portrayed in the carpeting spoke a great truth to me: centuries of faithful souls—St. Patrick, C. S. Lewis, Derick Bingham, and so many others—have left their footprint on Irish soil. And the great Lion has served as foundation and ruler of them all.

After procuring Queen's sweatshirts to take home for Kelsey and Langley, the three of us emerged from the Queen's student union to the swirling snowflakes of a snow globe. Snow continued well into the evening, so much so that we had to scrap any plans we had for a dinner out. So Cary has gone with Bill Stevenson, our Irish American friend and colleague, to fetch fish and chips for the small group of us residing at Lakeside. I have a romantic affinity for being "snowed in," and when it happens in Ireland, with laughing friends, fish and chips, and the Liverpool/Aston Villa football (soccer) match on television, it's all the better.

Day Five

Today has been a day graced with life-giving conversations. The more I look for places of resurrection on this journey, the more I see that they are most often to be found in the souls of folks who take the Greatest Commandment seriously: they love God deeply; they love people sacrificially.

Despite the heavy snowfall of last night, Nicola and two of her co-workers in Killyleagh, Billy and David, came to meet us in the Lakeside library for more summer mission planning. Sarah, Lakeside's cook, made hot blueberry and white chocolate scones for us, as well as the requisite hot tea. Our guests, who over the course of our two hours together never removed their coats and hats, ate and drank happily.

Nicola, Billy, and David are people I'd not known before this trip. Yet there is a clear kinship among us, a common desire to see the youth in Killyleagh touched by the love of Christ. I am always amazed at the instant bond between people who would, but for their shared love for God, be complete strangers. We ended our time today feeling positive about our next steps for the mission.

My afternoon schedule has been set for a while. Before leaving America I used Facebook to set up a time to see Deborah, a friend and former JBU colleague. Deborah is a citizen of Northern Ireland, but because she was born into a missionary family and educated abroad, she has an American accent. While she earned her Master's degree at JBU, she worked with us in student ministry. During that time she became very dear, and I was happy to have the chance to see her and hear about her life.

We met at a small coffee shop about a mile from Lakeside. As we drank our coffee and savored mince pies (which are only available at Christmas time), I quietly marveled at the peace and contentment that radiates from Deborah's countenance. The last time I saw Deborah she was visiting the States and openly confessed the difficulty she was having adapting to life in Northern Ireland. Transitions are hard; leaving friends behind in the States and getting re-established in a new country (even if it is your place of birth) is challenging. Today I see a new Deborah; she's lighthearted, at ease, and possesses a vision for future possibilities. On the icy sidewalk I hug her good-bye, grateful for the places of resurrection she has found and for the gift of her friendship.

This evening I see light shining out of darkness. Margaret Bingham has invited several of us from JBU for dinner at her home. Margaret is the widow of Derick (mentioned earlier), and she is as enthusiastic about JBU and its mission as Derick was. Her vivacious adult twin daughters, Kerrie and Claire, join us as well. We have a leisurely evening feasting on food and laughter while reminiscing about Derick. I am astonished at the peace in this family after great loss. Derick is missed, no doubt; but even so, there is palpable joy and hope in these women.

We spend the last thirty minutes of the evening browsing in Derick's library, which feels a bit like reading a person's diary. I smiled to see my own book, *Thin Places*, on the shelf; Derick had encouraged me as I wrote it, kindly submitting a blurb for the back cover. He was a prolific author, and on the wall hung a framed letter, hand-written and signed by President Bill Clinton, thanking Derick for one of his books that had provided encouragement after the Monica Lewinsky ordeal. I usually think of Derick as my friend and forget that his influence spanned the globe.

On our first night in Belfast, at the Christmas banquet, Margaret had come to me eager to say something. She recalled that Derick had been asked to present at a high-level academic conference in Oxford, and how he had been so keen to wear JBU regalia that day. It was my Master's hood that he borrowed for the occasion. I mailed it to him and he returned it immediately after the Oxford appearance. Margaret seemed to feel the need to mention that to me again. I was touched to know that it had meant something to Derick. Then she gave me a small book that had been published of Derick's reflections through the months of his illness, called *North of the Shadowlands*, the title clearly a nod to C. S. Lewis's own wanderings through the valley of the shadow.

Jesus said in Luke 20 that "He is not the God of the dead, but of the living, for to him all are alive." Resurrection punctuates and permeates the life of the Christian. I see it regularly on this journey.

Day Six

Cary and I are finally able to tour the cottages in Downpatrick to evaluate their usefulness for our mission team this summer. Getting there, however, is no easy task. Cary has driven in Britain many times, but it's always a trick to reorient to driving on the opposite side of the road and using the gear shift on the left rather than the right. And there is the additional variable of snow and ice on the roads. But we made it to Slievemoyle, the quintessentially Irish farm on the top of a hill just twenty minutes from Killyleagh.

Slievemoyle's proprietors are Greer and Maureen, who are Hadden Wilson's friends and members of his church. The cottages on their property seem ideal for our use and are absolutely charming. We stand outside in the wintery wind, marveling at the view of hillsides that roll down to the sea, the Isle of Man off in the distance. "Sometimes I imagine St. Patrick himself wandering over the hills of our property," Greer said. From what we know of Patrick, Greer's fanciful scene may be spot on.

Greer and Maureen invite us in for tea (of course), and we chat about our plans. Maureen is a warm spirit with a clear bent toward hospitality; Greer is jovial and chatty and the very image of actor Anthony Hopkins. We listen to them speak of their children and grandchildren in Australia and elsewhere, as well as the children they sponsor through world relief organizations whose pictures populate the front of their refrigerator. They have done mission and relief work in Bangkok and now sell Thai jewelry, which they display in the entryway of their home, for the benefit of the artists.

Paul wrote, "For God, who said, 'Let light shine out of darkness,' made his light shine in our hearts to give us the light of the knowledge of the glory of God in the face of Christ" (2 Corinthians 4:6). Cary and I leave Slievemoyle grateful for the provision of the cottages for our team and for Greer and Maureen, whose faces fairly glowed with "the light of the knowledge of God."

## Day Seven

We've just boarded a bus for the airport after a taxi ride from Lakeside. Our taxi driver was a friendly chap, even at the early hour. Conversing with strangers in Ireland is easier for me than it is at home in America. The conversations are enlightening and endearing.

The Psalmist urges us to "Come and see what God has done, how awesome his works in man's behalf!" (Psalm 66:5). This has been a good trip in many ways, one in which it was easy for me to "see the works of God." Not all journeys are that way. Some are fraught with frustration and disappointment, and it's harder to see the wonder of resurrection life in such circumstances. Yet the Psalmist says that God does wonderful works toward *all* people. We learn, by the grace of God, to have the eyes to see them.

# Humility

When I was a little girl, I wanted to be a nun when I grew up. My mother's family was Catholic; Mom made the switch to Protestantism when she married my Methodist father. During one of our visits with my grandmother and aunts in far off North Dakota, I learned that we had nuns in the family, distant aunts and cousins with peculiar names like "Sister Mulvina." Oh the curiosity, the novelty of their mysterious photos! In those days female monastics universally wore the formal habit—the long gown, the scapular, the veil, which I found intriguing. I envied their pretty beaded rosaries.

I had never actually met a nun, but that didn't matter. The mystique created by the black and white photographs before me was enough to make me know I wanted to be one. Until, that is, I learned that the nuns that wore the *white* habit (the one I liked best) were *nurses*. Well, even at age five I knew that I most certainly did not want to be a nurse. My romantic visions of becoming a nun went right out my vocational window.

The allure of monasticism, minus the concern about outfits, continues in adulthood as I have come to enjoy God in a more contemplative way. The monastery has woven its way into my own faith journey through contemplative retreats, spiritual direction, the writings of many wise Benedictines past and present, and my ongoing fascination with monastic life in medieval Celtic Ireland and Scotland.

I wrote much of this book while I was a scholar-in-residence at St. Benedict's monastery in St. Joseph, Minnesota. The sisters there provided a place for me to write in peace and solitude. They welcomed me into the rhythm of their daily communal prayers. Such is the hospitality of Benedictines all over the world, blessing visitors not only with food, shelter, and fellowship, but even more importantly, with space in which to listen to God.

During my time at St. Ben's, I learned a good deal about what it means to be a nun, or "sister," more appropriately. The sisters at St. Ben's are a joyful lot, and they greeted me daily with wide smiles, hearty hugs, and gentle assistance as I stumbled along in corporate prayer. They told me about the service projects and mission work they do around the world. I experienced the Benedictine value of hospitality first hand, as they welcomed me and others "as Christ." I enjoyed their beautiful gardens and pathways, felt at home in their carefully tended guesthouse, all a result of their conviction that it is important to take good care of what God has given.

What really captured my attention was that most of them are over sixty years old, many of them in their eighties. On the first day I was at St. Ben's, a handful of women celebrated their "Jubilee." Over seven hundred guests arrived to honor them for their fifty years of service and prayer at St. Ben's. *Fifty years of living and praying with the same group of women.* It made me wonder at the way we so easily move from congregation to congregation; few people today have worshipped with the same congregation for five years, much less fifty.

At my first meal at the monastery, a group of sisters enthusiastically invited me to join them at their dinner table. Each seemed eager to make my acquaintance. I learned that Sister Linda had earned a Ph.D. years ago and had been a top administrator at neighboring St. Benedict's College. Now retired, she continues to write, research, publish, and serve on the board of the scholars program from which I was benefiting. Another sister had multiple advanced degrees; another was an artist who had published a book of her work. Around the dinner table we went, the conversation growing more and more erudite with each chirpy personality. These women clearly did not approach retirement as a holiday, rather as an opportunity for mental rigor and vital service. Their faces glowed with life.

Lifelong learners inspire me with their attitude toward life and faith. In their accumulated wisdom, they are also the first to admit how much they don't know. Thomas Merton, spiritual writer and advisor to many, insisted that when it comes to prayer, we will always be beginners. This seems to contradict the biblical instruction to move away from the milk of infancy and dig our teeth into the meat of the Word of God. The Christian life is certainly about moving forward, being "transformed into the image of Christ for the sake of others," as Robert Mulholland suggests.

But in the midst of that growth process we realize humbly that we serve a God who is larger and more incomprehensible than we can imagine. Lifelong learners know that spiritual transformation does not happen in a year or a decade, but in the span of a lifetime. No matter what we might understand of God, he is always more. And no matter what we might learn about ourselves, there is always more.

This kind of humility is essential if we are to pursue a listening life. For how can we really hear if we're convinced we've already heard it all? "Humility," writes Thomas Kelly, "does not rest, in the final count, upon bafflement and discouragement and self-disgust at our shabby lives, a brow-beaten, dog-slinking attitude. It rests in the disclosure of the consummate wonder of God."

Luke Chapter 24 tells the story of two friends walking and talking on their way from Jerusalem to Emmaus. They are trying to help each other make sense of the events surrounding the crucifixion of Christ. I feel kinship with those two walkers because I routinely need someone to help me sort out the conundrums of my life. I like to imagine being a part of that conversation between the two friends walking to Emmaus. I love to have intense conversations about what God is up to.

Curiously, the resurrected Christ joins them, unrecognized. The two friends, with "faces downcast," relate the troubling recent events in Jerusalem to their fellow traveler. Their report to him is objectively correct. But apparently there is more to it, for Jesus finds it necessary to enlighten and correct their downcast spirits. All they've experienced had been foretold by the Scriptures. Jesus calls them "slow of heart" because their perspective is too narrow, and their perception is too limited.

Had these two friends responded in arrogance, rather than humility, they would have gone their way, leaving Jesus behind. Instead, their hearts and minds were attracted to this wise teacher. "Please, help us understand," I hear them saying. And in that desire for knowledge and clarity, "their eyes were opened, and they recognized him." They not only received understanding, they received the presence of Jesus. It was enough to make them start back on the seven-mile trek to Jerusalem to join the disciples, this time with a confident grasp of the miracles taking place around them. Walking and talking with a perceptive friend is a good way to practice a listening life.

Twice a year I take a small group of students to Subiaco Abbey, a men's monastery. The main purpose of the weekend is academic. Students read recommended texts prior to the trip, write reflective essays, and know that when it's over, they'll write a longer, in-depth paper. There is a spiritual objective as well. I know, confidently, that God will meet these students during their time at the monastery in ways that are unexpected and sometimes life-changing.

The weekend at the monastery is full of smashed presuppositions. No matter how well I prepare the students for the experience, they are always surprised. These students are evangelical Protestants, most of whom have never experienced a Catholic worship service, much less spent time with a group of men who have committed their life to a Catholic monastic community. We talk ahead of time about monastic values, about the monks' daily pattern of communal prayer, and about their founder, St. Benedict. Even so, I can see it in their eyes as we travel the three hours together in the university van: they can't believe anyone would actually *choose* a monastic life.

Subiaco Abbey sits castle-like on the crest of a hill in the Ozark mountains. The abbey church stands at the center, and the sight of its imposing Romanesque architecture sends a current of excitement through the van as we pull into the monastery parking lot. We disembark and enter through the doors of the retreat house where our accommodations are, and where we are are warmly welcomed by Carol, the retreat house hostess, and Brother Francis, the retreat director.

Carol could be any of these students' aunts or grandmothers, white-haired and smiling, genuinely pleased to see this group of young people with quizzical looks on their faces. Brother Francis, in his ankle-length, brown monk's habit, thinning hair and wire-rimmed glasses, looks very much the part of what these students imagined a monk to be.

But the similarity stops there; he's also wearing a baseball cap with a University of Kentucky team logo embroidered on it. The presupposition smashing begins.

Our weekend is spent joining the brothers in their daily rhythm of communal prayer: sunrise, early morning, noon, evening. Our assumptions about monastic life are challenged. Brother Francis cracks jokes as we walk together to prayers; a cantor's pitch is just a bit off in Vespers; brothers come into the Abbey church wearing street clothes, having ceased their daily labors for noon prayer. Heartfelt sincerity fills the audible prayers of the brothers. My students find the sincerity surprising, for they've assumed that so much praying every day would surely get a bit monotonous.

Each encounter with the brothers reveals a family of Christian men who pray, eat, and work together in ways that are so ordinary they become extraordinary. These are men who own little and need little. Amid their prayer and work, they find time for weekly gatherings for games and fun. They take time daily for *lectio divina*—sacred reading—but also attend the boys' academy basketball games. After seeing this, my students take back to campus a more accurate understanding of what it means to choose a monastic life. They admit, with a good dose of humility, that perhaps a life committed to prayer and community is both a difficult and an honorable vocation.

People who are listeners listen with the humble admission that their current understanding falls short of the fuller revelation. A listening life is perpetually aware that the glass we look through is only partially clear (1 Corinthians 13:12). It's healthy to wrestle with big questions, to mine for deeper truth and not settle for what merely lies on the surface. There are many trials for which we currently have no solutions, but they are safely held in the hands of God.

With open hearts, minds, eyes, and ears, we can continue to seek the Truth, knowing it will be given to us. And it will set us free.

# *Sources*

*Holy Bible,* New International Version. Grand Rapids, MI: Zondervan, 2006.


## Paying Attention

Johnson, Jan. *When the Soul Listens.* Colorado Springs, CO: NavPress, 1999.

Miller, Calvin. *Table of Inwardness.* Downers Grove, IL: InterVarsity Press, 1984.

Nouwen, Henri J. M. *The Only Necessary Thing: Living a Prayerful Life.* New York: Crossroad, 1999.


## Wonder

Christensen, Lars Lindberg, C. Sharkey, and R. Y. Shida. "Hubble." *NASA and the European Space Agency.* http://www.spacetelescope. org/.

Giglio, Louie. *Indescribable.* DVD Brentwood, TX: Sparrow Records, 2009.

Oliver, Mary. *Evidence: Poems.* Boston, MA: Beacon Press, 2010.

Shaw, Luci. *Harvesting Fog.* Montrose, CO: Pinyon Publishing, 2010.


## Illumination

Meehan, Bernard. *The Book of Kells.* London: Thames and Hudson, 1994.

Peterson, Eugene. *Eat This Book: A Conversation in the Art of Spiritual Reading.* Grand Rapids, MI: Eerdmans, 2006.

Saint John's Bible. "The Saint John's Bible." *Liturgical Press*. http:// www.saintjohnsbible.org/.

## Pain and People

Lewis, C. S. *Surprised by Joy: The Shape of My Early Life*. Boston, MA: Houghton Mifflin Harcourt, 1995.
Mason, Mike. *Practicing the Presence of People: How We Learn to Love*. Colorado Springs, CO: WaterBrook Press, 1999.

## Persistence, "Starry Night"

Foster, Richard. *Celebration of Discipline*, p. 1. New York: HarperCollins, 1981.
Norris, Kathleen. *Dakota: A Spiritual Geography*. Boston, MA: Houghton Mifflin, 1993.

## Sacramental Living

Foster, Richard. The Incarnational Tradition: Discovering the Sacramental Life, Chap. 7. In *Streams of Living Water*. New York: HarperCollins, 1998.
Shaw, Luci. *Water My Soul: Cultivating the Interior Life*. Grand Rapids, MI: Zondervan, 1998.

## Possessions

Bruno, Dave. "The 100 Thing Challenge." *Guy Named Dave*. http:// guynameddave.typepad.com/david_michael_bruno/.
Foster, Richard. *Freedom of Simplicity*. New York: HarperCollins, 1981.
St. Ignatius Loyola. *Spiritual Exercises of Saint Ignatius*. Trans. Anthony Mottola. New York: Doubleday, 1964.

## Silence and Stillness

Barton, Ruth Haley. *Invitation to Solitude and Silence: Experiencing God's Transforming Presence*. Downers Grove, IL: InterVarsity Press, 2004.

Jamison, Father Christopher. *Finding Sanctuary*. Collegeville, MN: Liturgical Press, 2006.

Kierkegaard, Søren and G. Pattison. *Spiritual Writings: A New Translation and Selection*. New York: Harber Perennial Modern Classics, 2010.

Nouwen, Henri. *The Way of the Heart*. New York: HarperCollins, 1981.

## Ancient Voices

à Kempis, Thomas. *The Imitation of Christ*. New Kensington, PA: Whitaker House, 1981.

Foster, Richard and J. B. Smith, Eds. *Devotional Classics*. New York: HarperCollins, 1990.

Kelly, Thomas. *A Testament of Devotion*. New York: HarperCollins, 1992.

Saint Benedict. *The Rule of Saint Benedict*. Ed. Timothy Fry. Collegeville, MN: The Liturgical Press, 1982.

Teresa of Ávila. *A Life of Prayer*, p. 46. Ed. James Houston. Portland, OR: Multnomah Press, 1983.

## When Listening is a Gift

Anderson, Keith and R. Reece. *Spiritual Mentoring: A Guide for Seeking and Giving Direction*. Downers Grove, IL: InterVarsity Press, 1999.

Julian of Norwich. *The Writings of Julian of Norwich*. Eds. Nicholas Watson and Jacqueline Jenkins. Belgium: Brepols, 2006.

Sellner, Edward. *The Celtic Soul Friend*. Notre Dame, IN: Ave Maria Press, 2002.

Simpson, Ray. *Soul Friendship: Celtic Insights Into Spiritual Mentoring*. London: Hodder & Stoughton, 1999.

## Compassion

Nouwen, J.M. *The Wounded Healer*. New York: Doubleday, 1972.
Paton, Alan. *Cry, the Beloved Country*. New York: Scribner, 2003.


## Journeying

Boers, Arthur Paul. *The Way is Made by Walking: A Pilgrimage Along the Camino de Santiago*. Downers Grove, IL: InterVarsity Press, 2007.
Cairns, Scott. *Short Trip to the Edge: Where Earth Meets Heaven–A Pilgrimage*. San Francisco: HarperSanFrancisco, 2007
Nouwen, J.M. *The Genessee Diary: Report from a Trappist Monastery*. New York: Doubleday, 1989.
Pemberton, Cintra. *Soulfaring: Celtic Pilgrimage Then and Now*. Harrisburg, PA: Morehouse Publishing, 1999.


## Humility

Fry, Timothy, Ed. *The Rule of St. Benedict*. Collegeville, MN: Liturgical Press, 1982.
Jamison, Abbot Christopher. *Finding Sanctuary: Monastic Steps for Everyday Life*. Collegeville, MN: Liturgical Press, 2006.
Kelly, Thomas. *A Testament of Devotion*, p. 35. New York: HarperCollins, 1992.
Mulholland, M. Robert. *Invitation to a Journey: A Roadmap for Spiritual Formation*. Downers Grove, IL: InterVarsity Press, 1993.
Norris, Kathleen. *The Cloister Walk*. New York: Riverhead Books, 1996.